Defoe

&

SPIRITUAL
AUTOBIOGRAPHY

Defoe

&

SPIRITUAL

AUTOBIOGRAPHY

BY G. A. STARR

PRINCETON, NEW JERSEY

PRINCETON UNIVERSITY PRESS

1965

52733

Copyright © 1965 by Princeton University Press
ALL RIGHTS RESERVED
L. C. Card: 66–10273

Publication of this book has been aided
by the Whitney Darrow Publication Reserve Fund
of Princeton University Press

Printed in the United States of America
by Kingsport Press, Inc., Kingsport, Tennessee

For Louis A. Landa

A historian of the novel, writing within the past decade, has this to say about *Robinson Crusoe*: "Here, in
his excursion into imaginary autobiography, Defoe had
nothing to guide him but his own genius. Indeed, the
phrase 'imaginary autobiography' is itself misleading if
it suggests that there were autobiographies extant
that Defoe could use as models. Apart from a few
works from remote periods, such as the *Confessions*
of St. Augustine, the prose literature of self-revelation
scarcely existed in Defoe's day." [1] In one respect this
view is clearly untenable: William Haller, William
York Tindall, Kenneth Murdock, and Margaret Bottrall have shown that a sizable literature of self-
revelation did exist in Defoe's day.[2] Yet the actual
nature and extent of Defoe's debt to autobiography,
and to spiritual autobiography in particular, have never
been assessed. It is the purpose of this study to do so:
to trace, in other words, a relationship which proves to
be important to the interpretation of Defoe's own
major fiction as well as to the larger problem of the
origins of the novel.

To emphasize certain affinities between *Robinson
Crusoe*, *Moll Flanders*, and the spiritual autobiography
is not to deny the relevance of other genres, such as

[1] Walter Allen, *The English Novel: A Short Critical History* (N.Y., 1954), pp. 26–27.
[2] *The Rise of Puritanism* (N.Y., 1938), p. 95f.; *John Bunyan,
Mechanick Preacher* (N.Y., 1934); *Literature & Theology in
Colonial New England* (Cambridge, Mass., 1949), p. 99f.;
*Every Man a Phoenix: Studies in Seventeenth-Century Auto-
biography* (London, 1958).

voyage literature and Newgate biography, whose contributions have been traced by various able scholars.[3] But research in these areas has involved what seems to me a disproportionate concern with outward narrative, and a corresponding neglect of its design or significance. The identification of specific sources has thrown valuable light on the range and fruitfulness of Defoe's reading, and on his achievement of verisimilitude through concrete detail; at the same time, it has fostered the belief that his artistry lies in the handling of individual episodes, rather than in the organization of such episodes to serve an overall purpose or to form a unified whole. By examining his narratives piecemeal, one lends weight to the notion that they are reducible to their component parts, that they form conglomerates rather than meaningful structures, and that they invite analysis but resist synthesis.

Without intending to minimize Defoe's indebtedness to the works that Secord and others have brought to our notice, I would suggest that *Robinson Crusoe*, and to a lesser extent *Moll Flanders* and *Roxana*, are as strongly influenced by a long tradition of spiritual autobiography. In the absence of any adequate survey, a preliminary sketch of this tradition seems not only necessary to my subsequent argument but desirable in

[3] See particularly Arthur W. Secord, *Studies in the Narrative Method of Defoe*, in *University of Illinois Studies in Language and Literature*, Vol. IX, No. 1 (Urbana, 1924). A similar approach to other works by Defoe may be found in Watson Nicholson, *The Historical Sources of Defoe's Journal of the Plague Year* (Boston, 1919); John Robert Moore, *Defoe's Sources for "Robert Drury's Journal,"* in *Indiana University Humanities Series*, No. 9 (Bloomington, 1943). See also p. 126, n. 1 below.

itself.[4] The opening chapter focuses on those aspects of the genre that bear on Defoe, so that comprehensiveness is not its aim, although the generalizations rest on a number of representative texts. Since certain little-known works are discussed in detail, and others that have become classics are alluded to only in passing, it may be helpful to indicate briefly some principles that have guided my selection.

In the first place, various works are cited which existed only in manuscript during Defoe's lifetime. The probability that Defoe did not know a given autobiography is no reason for excluding it from this study, since his indebtedness to an entire genre, not to specific works, is to be demonstrated. It was customary, of course, for spiritual diaries and memoirs to circulate in manuscript, so he may have known some works long before they were printed. Such material is cited here because it expresses a common theme with particular clarity or force, not on the bare possibility that Defoe might have seen it.

Secondly, a number of different autobiographies are cited to illustrate certain themes, and several works are examined at some length. It would have been possible to document each point from a different work: the

---

[4] Spiritual autobiography is treated only briefly in two valuable recent studies: see Wayne Shumaker, *English Autobiography: Its Emergence, Materials and Form* (Berkeley and Los Angeles, 1954), and Roy Pascal, *Design and Truth in Autobiography* (Cambridge, Mass., 1960). Cf. also Georges Gusdorf's interesting essay, "Conditions et limites de l'autobiographie," in *Formen der Selbstdarstellung*, edited by Günter Reichenkron (Berlin, 1956), pp. 105–23. Anna Robeson Burr's *Religious Confessions and Confessants* (Boston and N.Y., 1914) is more directly concerned with spiritual autobiography, but less illuminating.

resulting cloud of witnesses would help suggest the high degree of uniformity between spiritual autobiographies, but would obscure the fact that they are at the same time personal records. If followed exclusively, then, this approach would convey the conventional quality of the genre, but would conceal the element of individuality present in even the most stereotyped autobiography. On the other hand, every point could have been documented by discussing only a few chosen works. This approach runs the opposite risk, for it is apt to exaggerate the individuality of each writer. The fewer the subjects examined, the greater the tendency to heighten their idiosyncrasies, and to account psychologically for details that are in fact symbolic and conventional.[5] This book seeks to avoid both extremes by combining extensive citation from a wide range of works with close analysis of a few: the objective is a picture of uniformity amid diversity, of individuality within convention.

In the third place, little is said here about Quaker and Baptist autobiographies. My impression is that they gave rise not to fiction but to further Quaker and Baptist autobiographies. My reason for omitting them, however, is not that they are unlikely to have influenced Defoe, for the same objection could be made against manuscript evidence which I do use. Rather, they are excluded in order to make clear that spiritual autobiography was the common property of English Protestantism, not the private domain of enthusiasts. Such studies as *John Bunyan, Mechanick Preacher* have fostered the belief that spiritual autobiography flourished only on the sectarian fringes of seventeenth-

[5] See below, p. 61, n. 12.

century religious life. Mr. Tindall's book gives the entire genre a somewhat disreputable air,[6] and tends to hide the fact that many spiritual autobiographers were more sophisticated and conservative, both doctrinally and stylistically, than the Baptists and Ranters whom it treats. By drawing on Presbyterians and Anglicans for my evidence, I try to indicate the range—social and temperamental as well as denominational—that spiritual autobiography actually embraced. By extension, I seek to show that many of Defoe's religious attitudes are less distinctively or exclusively Puritan than they are commonly taken to be.

This aim has also influenced my selection of illustrative material from the non-autobiographical religious literature of the period. Traditional source-studies, attempting to trace specific narrative details, must face in some form the problem of what Defoe actually read. Such questions have little relevance here, however, for in no case is it alleged that Defoe must have gone to this or that source for a particular idea. Instead, my method is to show wherever possible that he would have encountered an idea in a multitude of autobiographies, sermons, and practical works. By a comparison of statements made in different contexts, in different decades, by authors of different denominations, it becomes clear that the leading religious ideas in Defoe's fiction were in fact commonplaces of the English Protestant tradition, not merely crotchets of his much-discussed Dissenting milieu.

With this in mind, I cite Anglican divines as often as Nonconformists: since my argument does not de-

[6] For a more sympathetic account, see Roger Sharrock's excellent introduction to Bunyan's *Grace Abounding* (Oxford, 1962).

pend on Defoe's actually having heard or read them,
the words of a Bishop are no less appropriate than
those of a Bartholomean. By the same token, the statements of a Tillotson or Baxter carry little more weight
than those of the many lesser divines who are also
quoted. It is true that the views of distinguished writers
and preachers constantly reappear in the works of
their less gifted brethren; thus we find not only the
thoughts but the very phrases of a Sibbes or Taylor
echoed in provincial pulpits. It follows that one might
document homiletic commonplaces from the works of
influential divines exclusively. Here again, however, a
compromise has been attempted: some of the leading
religious figures of the period appear prominently, but
their testimony is supported and amplified by that of
obscurer men.

A number of ideas discussed here can be traced to
earlier works; many of them are to be found in Augustine, for instance, where they were reasonably acces-
sible to the seventeenth-century reader. If a contemporary divine is quoted instead, it is not necessarily
because he expresses an idea as well as Augustine, but
because he shows it being rethought and recirculated
in his own day. In some cases I do indicate the remoter
backgrounds of a motif, especially when it is Biblical
in origin. But I am often content to cite only seventeenth-century versions of themes that actually origi-
nate with the Fathers, or the Schoolmen, or the Reformers, since my primary aim is to show the form in
which they were current during Defoe's lifetime. Furthermore, theological trends in the Restoration have
been studied somewhat less intensively than those of
the preceding period: owing to the comparative neglect
of later developments, the relationships between Non-

conformity and earlier Puritanism on the one hand, and contemporary Anglicanism on the other, are still only partially understood. In the hope of throwing some light on these problems, I confine my discussion of doctrine largely to the Restoration period, although fully aware that in many cases a belief or its mode of expression has a long ancestry.

In citing Defoe's fiction, I have used George A. Aitken's edition of *The Romances and Narratives of Daniel Defoe*, 16 vols. (London, 1903), except where otherwise indicated; I chose this edition primarily to facilitate reference to two works not included in the Shakespeare Head Edition, *Due Preparations for the Plague* and *Serious Reflections during the Life and Surprising Adventures of Robinson Crusoe*.

I am grateful to the Union and Princeton Theological Seminaries for access to their McAlpin and Puritan collections, and to Princeton University for the fellowships that made my research possible. I should like to thank Professors Henry K. Miller, Norman Grabo, and Wayne Shumaker for generous guidance on various topics; I have received helpful criticism and advice from Professor Maximillian Novak, and I am indebted to Professor Benjamin Boyce for a number of valuable suggestions. I also appreciate deeply the personal kindness as well as the editorial skill of Miss Miriam Brokaw of Princeton University Press. My greatest obligations are to Professor Landa and to my wife.

G.A.S.

Berkeley, May 1965

CONTENTS

Defoe

&

SPIRITUAL
AUTOBIOGRAPHY

Spiritual Autobiography

To compose any kind of autobiography is to assume
one's own importance. In the seventeenth century,
only the spiritual autobiographer could avoid the awk-
wardness of having to justify this assumption. All
other autobiographers felt obliged to vindicate their
choice of subject, and to demonstrate (or at least
assert) that their material—they themselves—deserved
attention. "Certainly it will be found much better,"
says Lord Herbert of Cherbury in the opening sentence of his autobiography, "for men to guide themselves by such observations as their father, grandfather, and great grandfather might have delivered to
them, than by those vulgar rules and examples, which
cannot in all points so exactly agree unto them." [1] Such
usefulness to one's heirs was a frequent justification of
autobiography, so frequent, in fact, that a humble man
like Walter Pringle might well pause, in composing his
own, to admit that "some may think it strange that I
should adventure to leave anything in write, though it
be only to my children, in this wise age, wherein very
much wisdom, learning, and piety, is to be found in
books. Some of these being also written by fathers to

[1] *The Life of Edward Lord Herbert of Cherbury. Written
by Himself* (London, 1770), pp. 1-2. In all subsequent foot-
notes the place of publication, unless otherwise indicated, is
London.

their children, full of many useful instructions and prudent rules for them to order their life by in their greatest concernments . . . so that though I were able, yet it were needless for me to add anything of that kind, since you, my dear children, may read the best of these." [2] Other autobiographers alleged different motives for recording their experiences and observations; to judge by the usual opening remarks, a variety of powerful but disinterested impulses could overcome a man's natural reticence. In any case, the very act of writing one's apologia demanded apology, unless one's spiritual life was to be the subject.

That one's "soul-experiences" are fit to write about was an assumption needing no justification. The entire Reformation tended to stress the importance of the spiritual welfare of the individual. The conviction that every man is both enabled and obliged to scrutinize his own soul was widely shared, whether one regards the attitude as distinctively "Puritan," with Haller, or finds it typical of the entire English Protestant outlook, as do the Georges.[3] This combined sense of privilege and responsibility in an all-important undertaking is well expressed by Oliver Heywood, as he sets out to write his autobiography: "Since the god of the spirits of al flesh hath breathed into me the breath of life and made me a living soul, since he hath put into

[2] "The Memoirs of Walter Pringle of Greenknow; or some few of the free mercies of God to him, and his will to his children, left to them under his own hand," in *Select Biographies*, edited for the Wodrow Society by the Rev. W. K. Tweedie, 2 vols. (Edinburgh, 1845–1847), I, 479–80.

[3] William Haller, *The Rise of Puritanism* (N.Y., 1938), *passim;* Charles H. and Katherine George, *The Protestant Mind of the English Reformation 1570–1640* (Princeton, 1961); on the role of "personalism," see p. 29 f.

my soul that godlike reflecting faculty of conscience, since also he hath so frequently called upon me to descend into mine oune hart, to commune therewith, to search and try my wayes, to examine my selfe, to proue my worke, I desire as the lord wil helpe me to deal freely, plainly, & ingeniously with my selfe in so weighty & necessary a busines as this is that concernes the weal or woe of my immortal soul to al eternity." [4] Implicit in this statement is the Protestant view that no earthly mediation, no clerical intercession can affect the weal or woe of one's immortal soul, but that one's own exertions can and must influence it. Heywood finds God near at hand, approachable, demanding to be dealt with openly and directly; such belief gives strong impetus to self-examination and self-revelation, and makes it only natural that autobiography should be regarded as weighty and necessary business.

Since every man is responsible for the well-being of his own soul, he must mark with care each event or stage in its development. As his own spiritual physician, he must duly note every symptom of progress or relapse; after all, his case is one of life or death. The need for constant, almost clinical self-analysis was generally recognized. Heywood is again typical in declaring himself bound "to compare my past and present state and obserue my proficiency in christianity, to see whether I be better this year then the last, whether grace be stronger, corruptions weaker, my hart more soft, conscience more tender, wil more

[4] *The Rev. Oliver Heywood, B.A., 1630–1702; His Autobiography, Diaries, Anecdote and Event Books; Illustrating the General and Family History of Yorkshire and Lancashire,* edited by J. Horsfall Turner, 3 vols. (Bingley, 1881–1883), I, 133.

bowed, rectifyed, resolved, and my life more re-
formed." [5] Heywood's urge to determine whether he is
"better this year then the last" suggests that self-
analysis was a continuous, or at least regular, process.
This was in fact the case, so that spiritual autobiography tended to be a summing-up and review of a
whole series of self-dissections. As a further consequence, diary-keeping frequently proved helpful in
documenting and compiling one's spiritual case-
history. A diary not only supplied the prospective
autobiographer with a record of his spiritual fortunes;
it developed in him the habit of observing and interpreting every outward and inward occurrence for
the sake of its spiritual significance. For these and other
reasons, diary-keeping was a highly recommended
spiritual exercise. The value of a diary was summed up
by Joseph Williams in his own diary as follows:

"I shall never excel while I neglect meditation, self-
examination, and the recording of remarks on
myself. . . . Surely, singular advantages must follow
such a practice, for hereby I may observe something of
God to my soul, and of my soul to God:—I may pour
out my soul to God accordingly, and be either humble
or thankful:—I may judge how it is with me in respect
of time past; and, whether I have profited, by grace, to
find out the means whereby I have profited, that I may

[5] *Autobiography*, I, 151. For self-scrutiny as a clinical process, see Thomas Watson's *Christian Soldier* (N.Y., 1810; 1st
edition, 1669), p. 47: "Self-searching is an heart-anatomy. As
a Chirurgeon, when he makes a dissection in the body, discovers the *intestina*, the inward parts, the heart, liver, arteries:
so a Christian anatomizeth himself; he searcheth what is flesh,
and what is spirit; what is sin, and what is grace." Cf. also
John Howe's Preface to John Corbet's *Self-Employment in
Secret* (Philadelphia, n.d.; 1st edition, 1681), pp. 8–9.

make more constant use of such means; or, where I have been negligent, to observe by what temptation I was overcome, that my former errors may make me more wary for the future;—besides many other benefits which I may, by the Lord's help, derive from a diary." [6]

Williams is evidently sincere, but what is one to make of the discovery that his remarks largely paraphrase a commendation of diaries first published sixty-five years earlier? Far from lessening the weight of his testimony, the fact that he should find Isaac Ambrose's arguments of 1650 entirely valid and appropriate in 1715 seems to me remarkable evidence of the importance attached to diary-keeping throughout the period.[7]

It was a matter of personal choice, of course, whether keeping a diary should be the specific means of regular and methodical self-inspection. But the object of a diary—to regard and weigh spiritually every episode in one's life—presented itself as a duty, not an option. It was a duty sanctioned in the first place by thankfulness. "Indeed what is our whole life," asks John Beadle in his *Journal or Diary of a Thankful Christian*, "but a continued deliverance? We are daily delivered, either from the violence of the creature, or the rage of men, or the treachery of our own hearts; either our houses are freed from firing, or goods from

---

[6] *An Enlarged Series of Extracts from the Diary, Meditations and Letters of Mr. Joseph Williams of Kidderminster*, edited by Benjamin Hanbury (1815), pp. 13–14.

[7] The remarks of Isaac Ambrose on diary-keeping appear in *Media: The Middle Things*, along with specimens of his own diary between 1641 and 1649. The passage in question is quoted by W. L. Sachse in his introduction to the diary of Roger Lowe, pp. 2–3 (see below, n. 24).

plundering, or our bodies from danger, or our names from reproaches, or our souls from snares." [8] Gratitude obliges one to observe and acknowledge such deliverance; failure to do so slights Providence, adding practical atheism to ingratitude. In this light, the task Richard Baxter sets himself in his autobiography is a necessary one: "As Travellers and Seamen use to do after great Adventures and Deliverances, I hereby satisfie my Conscience, in praising the Blessed Author of all those undeserved Mercies which have filled up my Life." [9] Heywood feels himself under the same obligation. Wherever he has discovered "any special appearances of god upon my hart or in my life," he proposes to "owne and honour god therin, and for them." "I would not be the graue of enjoyments," he says, "but would ingage my life to fruitfulnes and desire god would inlarge my hart in suitable thankfulnes." [10] Lucy Hutchinson likewise declares at the beginning of her memoirs: "I thought it might be a means to stir up my thankfulness for things past, and to encourage my faith for the future, if I recollected as much as I have heard or can remember of the passages of my youth, and the general and particular provi-

[8] Quoted by Haller, *Rise of Puritanism*, p. 97; cf. Bishop Rainbow's meditation on April 20, 1681, in *The Life of the Right Reverend Father in God, Edw. Rainbow, D.D. Late Lord Bishop of Carlisle* [by Jonathan Banks] (1688); and George Brysson's prefatory remarks in *Memoirs of Mr. William Veitch, and George Brysson, Written by Themselves*, edited by Thomas McCrie (Edinburgh, 1825), p. 267.

[9] *Reliquiae Baxterianae, Or, Mr. Richard Baxter's Narrative of The Most Memorable Passages of his Life and Times. Faithfully Publish'd from his own Original Manuscript, by Matthew Sylvester* (1696), p. 136.

[10] Heywood, *Autobiography*, I, 151; cf. John Flavel, *Divine Conduct*, in his *Whole Works*, 2 vols. (Glasgow, 1754), II, 113.

dences exercised to me, both in the entrance and progress of my life." [11] In some instances the very titles and epigraphs of memoirs and autobiographies indicate the motif of thankfulness. John Coad calls the vivid account of his sufferings and deliverances in connection with Monmouth's rebellion "A Memorandum of the Wonderful Providences of God to a poor unworthy Creature," and Sir Robert Sibbald, founder of the Royal College of Physicians at Edinburgh, opens his memoirs with the inscription, "Come and hear, all ye that fear God, and I will declare what he hath done for my soul" (Psalm 66:16). [12]

Regarding and weighing spiritually each episode in one's life was a duty sanctioned, in the second place, by prudence. Time, it was felt, is a precious commodity, to be rationed and redeemed through vigilant attention to its expenditure. In this spirit, Matthew Henry devoted a course of sermons to the text, "See then that ye walk circumspectly, not as fools, but as wise, redeeming the time, because the days are evil." "This day," he writes in November 1690, "I concluded my subject of redeeming time, from Ephes.

[11] "The Life of Mrs. Lucy Hutchinson," in *Memoirs of the Life of Colonel Hutchinson*, edited by Julius Hutchinson, revised by C. H. Firth (1906), p. 1.

[12] *A Memorandum of the Wonderful Providences of God to a poor unworthy Creature* (1849); *The Memoirs of Sir Robert Sibbald (1641–1722)*, edited by F. P. Hett (Oxford, 1932), p. 49. The verse from Psalm 66 also occurs as an epigraph to Richard Kilby's *Hallelv-iah: Praise yee the Lord, for the Vnburthening of a loaden Conscience: By his Grace in Iesus Christ vouchsafed unto the worst sinner of all the whole world* (Cambridge, 1618); to Jane Turner's *Choice Experiences Of The kind dealings of God before, in, and after Conversion* (1653); to the *Memoirs of Mr. William Veitch;* and to *A Narration of the Life of Mr. Henry Burton* (1643).

5:16; and, among other things, directed as very useful, to keep a short account every night how the day has been spent. This will discover what are the thieves of our time, and will show us what progress we make in holiness." [13] Parents often gave their children similar instructions. Ralph Thoresby, who was to become a famous antiquary and F.R.S., went up to London in 1677 at the age of nineteen; his first letter from home urges him to "Remember what I advised you, to be always employed in some lawful employment or other." His father suggests several, and adds: "I would have you, in a little book, which you may either buy or make of two or three sheets of paper, take a little journal of any thing remarkable every day, principally as to yourself, as, suppose, Aug. 2. I was at such a place; (or) . . . such a one preached from such a text, and my heart was touched; (or) I was a negligent hearer, (or) otherwise, &c. I have thought this a good method for one to keep a good tolerable decorum in actions, &c. because he is to be accountable to himself as well as to God, which we are too apt to forget." [14]

Henry's stress on accounting for time spent and the elder Thoresby's view of life as accountable are typical in their very phraseology: exhortations to self-examination were often expressed in distinctly mercantile terms. This is not surprising in an age which

[13] Sir John B. Williams, *Memoirs of the Life, Character and Writings of the Rev. Matthew Henry* (Boston, 1830), p. 92. Henry concludes, "and now, why should not I make the experiment?" and from this time he did keep a fairly minute and regular diary.

[14] *The Diary of Ralph Thoresby, F.R.S., Author of the Topography of Leeds (1677–1724)*, edited by the Rev. Joseph Hunter, 2 vols. (1830), 1, xv. Cf. Heywood, *Autobiography*, 1, 159–60.

saw nothing ludicrous or profane in the description of
a holy man as "a spiritual Merchant in an heavenly
Exchange, driving a rich Trade for the treasures of the
other world." [15] After all, English Protestantism had
repudiated the monkish ideal of otherworldliness, and
insisted instead on the compatibility of earthly and
spiritual callings. As a result, utterly mundane activities could be drawn upon to illustrate and enforce
religious duties. In his *Christian Directions*, Thomas
Gouge uses a very popular argument for the importance of self-examination: "As he is the best Tradesman that every day in the Evening taketh an account
of his worldly losses and gains; so he is the best
Christian that every day in the Evening taketh an
account of his spiritual losses and gains, whether he go
forward or backward in the ways of Godliness." [16]
Observation of trade confirms Mrs. Hulton, one of

[15] James Janeway, *Invisibles, Realities, Demonstrated in the
Holy Life and Triumphant Death of Mr. John Janeway* . . .
(1684), p. 42. The source of the image is alluded to by
Thomas Gouge in *The Young Man's Guide. Through the
Wilderness of this World, to the Heavenly Canaan. Shewing
him how to carry himself Christian-like in the whole course
of his Life* (1680), p. 42: "Believers are *Merchants*, Matth.
13:45, *Merchant-adventurers*, that will adventure all they
have, their whole Stock and Patrimony, for the riches of that
good Land."

[16] *Christian Directions, Shewing how to Walk with God All
the Day long* (1679), p. 84. The analogy is developed at
length in John Shower's *Serious Reflections on Time and
Eternity* (Glasgow, 1828; 1st edition, 1689), pp. 151–52; in a
letter "On a Tradesman's casting up his Shop" in "Memoirs of
Mrs. Elizabeth Bury," in *Memoirs of Eminently Pious
Women of the British Empire*, edited by Thomas Gibbon,
revised by Samuel Burder, 3 vols. (1827), 1, 382–83; cf.
[Richard Allestree], *Whole Duty of Man* (1658), Sunday V,
Par. 28. On this matter see Max Weber, *The Protestant Ethic
and the Spirit of Capitalism* (N.Y., 1958), pp. 123–25.

Matthew Henry's sisters, in the same opinion. Just as a shop must be constantly attended though perhaps for some time no profits come in; so "the trade of religion must still be followed, though there be not, for the present, any sensible comfort and benefit." [17] This "trade of religion" metaphor, although it could serve on occasion to warn against spiritual bankruptcy (as in sermons on the unprofitable servant or the wages of sin), was most often used to emphasize the riches attending diligent spiritual enterprise. Thus the biography of John Janeway shows a man reckoning up and truly relishing his (spiritual) opulence. In his diary, we are told, Janeway "took notice what incomes and profit he received, in his spiritual traffique; what returns from that far-country": this agreeable exercise "left a sweet calm upon his spirits, because he every night made even his accounts; and if his sheets should prove his winding sheet, it had been all one." [18] Thus the imagery of spiritual traffic was by no means confined to the plane of petty shop-keeping. Thomas Lye, one of the preachers at Dr. Annesley's Cripplegate Exercises, strikes a similar note, suitable to the ambitious commercial undertakings of his London

[17] Sir John B. Williams, *Memoirs of the Life and Character of Mrs. Sarah Savage . . . of Mrs. Anne Hulton and Mrs. Eleanor Radford . . . by their Brother, Matthew Henry* (Philadelphia, n.d.), p. 265. In this work and the *Memoirs of Matthew Henry* cited above (n. 13), Williams is in part author, in part editor; I have quoted only passages written by the Henrys themselves.

[18] *Invisibles, Realities. . .* , p. 59; cf. Joseph Hall, *The Third Century of Meditations and Vows*, No. xxxii, in his *Works*, edited by Philip Wynter, 10 vols. (Oxford, 1863), vii, 499. For the "trade of religion" metaphor used negatively, as warning rather than promise, see Thomas Watson, *Christian Soldier*, p. 49.

audience. Faith, he proclaims, "discovers a world beyond the moon, and trades thither; leaving the men of the earth to load themselves with clay and coals, faith pursues its staple commodity, and traffics for grace and glory." [19] In short, the familiar routines and rewards of commerce, whether on a modest or grandiose scale, served to illustrate effectively the nature and value of spiritual exercise. Throughout the period, variations on this analogy, grotesque as it may seem to some today, enforced spiritual duties by bringing them, as it were, home to men's business and bosoms.

Several other assumptions gave impetus and direction to the writing of autobiography. One was the principle that there are universal and recurrent elements in human affairs, particularly in vicissitudes of the soul. History repeats itself not only in man's outward, group existence, but in the spiritual life of individuals. Circumstances vary, but only accidentally or superficially: however much they may obscure basic similarities from the casual observer, on closer view they actually confirm and heighten the constant, general features of religious experience.

Such a belief naturally promoted the writing and reading of spiritual autobiographies. A man need not have done anything remarkable in the eyes of the world for his autobiography to be worthwhile; or, if

[19] "How are we to live by Faith on Divine Providence?" in *The Morning Exercises at Cripplegate, St. Giles in the Fields, and in Southwark: being Divers Sermons, preached A.D. MDCLIX-MDCLXXXIX*, edited by Samuel Annesley, 5th edition, 6 vols. (1844), I, 385 (hereafter referred to as *Cripplegate Exercises*). Cf. also Bartholomew Ashwood, *The Heavenly Trade or the Best Merchandizing: the only way to live well in impoverishing times* (1679); Christopher Jelinger, "The Spirituall Merchant," in *Three Treatises* (n.p., 1676).

his spiritual life did happen to be unique in its circumstances, or extraordinary in its intensity, it would nevertheless correspond with that of all other Christians, and be meaningful to them for this very reason. Thus Thomas Halyburton says of his autobiography, "should the book ever fall into the hands of any other Christian, it may not prove unuseful to him, considering that the work of the Lord, in substance, is uniform and the same in all; and 'as face answereth to face in a glass,' so does one Christian's experience answer to another's, and both to the word of God." [20] Halyburton's assured tone may be contrasted with the slightly defensive remarks of Herbert of Cherbury quoted earlier. Lord Herbert, recording his overt deeds and words on specific occasions, could hope to benefit only those who might find themselves in analogous situations. Halyburton, recording the "work of the Lord" within himself, expected to help all Christians, since their situations must agree in substance.

So strong was this belief in the essential uniformity and sameness of Christian experience that occasionally it could inhibit spiritual autobiography. This seems, at any rate, to have been the case with Baxter, who says: "for any more particular Account of Heart-Occurrences, and God's Operations on me, I think it somewhat unsavory to recite them; seeing God's Dealings are much what the same with all his Servants in the main, and the Points wherein he varieth are usually so small, that I think not such fit to be repeated: Nor have I any thing extraordinary to glory in, which is not common to the rest of my Brethren, who have the

---

[20] *Memoirs of the Rev. Thomas Halyburton* [1674–1712], *Professor of Divinity in the University of St. Andrews* (Princeton, 1833), p. 57.

same Spirit, and are Servants of the same Lord." [21]
Baxter's diffidence is exceptional. His primary concern
in the *Reliquiae*, however, is with public affairs, in
which he had been deeply involved both as an influential actor and as a vulnerable observer. The self-
appraisal in this work is acute, but deals mainly with
his responses to ideas, men, and events. The book does
reveal, as one critic observes, a strong impulse on
Baxter's part to talk about himself and his intimate
concerns,[22] but only about those concerns or aspects of
himself which he feels others are entitled or enabled to
judge. Whether Baxter was intent on vindicating or
merely documenting his public career, it was this
rather than his soul's career that he preferred to discuss; he evidently chose to keep to himself his dealings
with God. Not that he slighted such dealings, or
accounts of them: his practical works analyze them in
great detail, but not in the first person singular. To do
so would be "somewhat unsavory"—would smack of
egotism or downright enthusiasm; and whatever else
the *Reliquiae* may be, it is Baxter's sustained attempt to
clear himself and his party from the taint of self-
assertive excess. His refusal to give a "particular
Account of Heart-Occurrences" should probably be
regarded in this light. At any rate, the conviction that
spiritual experience follows much the same pattern in
all men is borne out by Baxter's testimony, even

---

[21] *Reliquiae*, p. 124.
[22] Margaret Bottrall, *Every Man a Phoenix: Studies in
Seventeenth-Century Autobiography* (1958), p. 117. In the
preface to his biography of his wife, Baxter characteristically
concludes that "publick things are fittest for publick notice":
see *A Breviate of the Life of Margaret, The Daughter of
Francis Charlton, of Apply in Shropshire, Esq; And Wife of
Richard Baxter* (1681), sig. [A3ʳ].

though he declines to act on it in the usual manner.

Further evidence that this conviction was widely held may be found in the preface to the memoirs of Ambrose Barnes. Describing the composition of the work, the anonymous author says: "Here are also sundry passages out of many written lives that are passant amongst us, but I protest before God . . . there is not one lineament, not one fine stroke applyed to this gentleman, out of the printed lives of any holy upright persons that have fallen in my way, that in my conscience I believed not to be very just, and wherein I had not an exact and rigid respect to truth." [23] The notion that spiritual biography can be assembled from "interchangeable parts," with no loss of truthfulness or accuracy, at once illustrates and applies the principle that the life of the spirit is the same in all men. The process of adaptation and assimilation, here so frankly acknowledged, went on more or less consciously in the writing of spiritual autobiography as well. This practice had important consequences, to be discussed later, for the growth of fiction. At this point it is sufficient to note its implications for autobiography itself.

In the first place, it led to highly conventional descriptions of heart-occurrences. Modern critics seldom fail to notice this quality in diaries and autobiographies of the period, and they almost invariably deplore it. The editor of one diary, for instance, laments that its author will "periodically express his feelings, whether downcast or fearful or jubilant, in

[23] *Memoirs of the Life of Mr. Ambrose Barnes, Late Merchant and Sometime Alderman of Newcastle upon Tyne* [1627–1710], edited by W. H. D. Longstaffe, *Surtees Society Publications*, Vol. L (1867), p. 17. Written in 1716, this work presents an interesting picture of the changing complexion of Dissent in the early eighteenth century.

passages of a semi-biblical style, introspective enough in character, but so stereotyped as to minimize their value to any psychologist who might try to reconstruct Lowe's mind." [24] He does allow that "hackneyed as these entries are, they ring with an unmistakable earnestness," but fails to solve, or even to see, the paradox in this. Ordinarily, to be sure, emotions will be diluted or distorted by a stereotyped and hackneyed mode of expressing them; on the other hand, conventional phraseology can actually enhance the description of feelings or experiences noteworthy for their universality rather than their uniqueness. Spiritual autobiography happens to dwell on feelings and experiences of this latter sort. As stated earlier, it attaches significance to what all Christians have felt and undergone, and disregards or suppresses idiosyncrasies except as they illustrate typical stages or predicaments in the soul's development. In this light, the traditional idiom seems entirely appropriate: it amplifies the rendering of individual experience by associating it with the experience of all Christians. In short, the spiritual autobiographer naturally found himself thinking "what oft was thought," and since he felt that it had been "ne'er so well express'd" as in the Bible, he was content to employ the same imagery and turns of phrase. Little wonder that the psychologist, in search of revealing peculiarities, finds many religious diaries and autobiographies of limited value.

In the second place, the belief that spiritual life varies little from man to man, with its corollary that descriptions of such experience are somewhat inter-

[24] William L. Sachse, introduction to *The Diary of Roger Lowe of Ashton-in-Makerfield, Lancashire 1663–74* (New Haven, 1938), p. 10.

changeable, enabled every man to measure his own spiritual state by that of others. In performing the constant self-scrutiny required of him, the individual Christian was assisted by all accounts of similar endeavors. He might recognize and rejoice in his own tokens of grace and election by reading of them in others; or, through the writings of others, he might be startled out of reprobate habits by discovering their symptoms and aftermath. On the way to salvation, he would pass through certain recognizable stages, and the route to damnation was mapped out for him in equal detail. The voyage had long been a popular metaphor for the object and rigors of spiritual aspiration, and will be considered in more detail below; here the point is that a man could tell which way he was headed, and how far he had come, by consulting the signposts and milestones set up for his guidance in spiritual autobiographies. By means of them, he could discover the spiritual connotation of seemingly indifferent events, and read a meaning for himself in external, prosaic happenings.

Haller has spoken of the tendency of "the Puritan faith" to invest "the most trivial circumstances of the most commonplace existence with the utmost significance." [25] That Puritans alone were endowed (or infested) with this frame of mind is doubtful, but in any case it was an outlook fostered by constantly comparing the spiritual vicissitudes of others with one's own. No "commonplace existence" was without its share of spiritual trials and temptations, and no "trivial circumstances" were to be despised as calls to conversion or marks of election. The most ordinary and inconsequential things, as one divine points out, "may be

[25] *Rise of Puritanism*, p. 97.

an occasion to set people on thinking, and reflecting upon their state and their actions, and so they may proceed to an accusing or excusing of themselves." "Conscience," this writer continues, "is something so watchful and busy, that it may be alarmed and set on work by things, I will not say how small and inconsiderable in themselves." [26] The hazards of neglecting the trivial are described eloquently by Jeremy Taylor; asserting that sins eventually "destroy the soul by their abode, who at their first entry might have been killed with the pressure of a little finger," he reflects "so have I seen the little purls of a spring sweat through the bottom of a bank, and intenerate the stubborn pavement till it hath made it fit for the impression of a child's foot; and it was despised, like the descending pearls of a misty morning, till it had opened its way, and made a stream large enough to carry away the ruins of the undermined strand, and to invade the neighbouring gardens; but then the despised drops were grown into an artificial river, and an intolerable mischief." [27] Since mere trifles can have the gravest consequences if allowed to pass unheeded, it follows that nothing is beneath the notice of an alert Christian. The prudent man draws warning or encouragement

[26] Samuel Wright, *A Treatise on the Deceitfulness of Sin; And its Leading Men to Hardness of Heart: With the Means Appointed To prevent both its Hardning and Deceiving*, 5th edition (1735), p. 108.

[27] "Of Growth in Sin; or, the several states and degrees of sinners," in *The Whole Works of the Right Reverend Jeremy Taylor*, edited by Reginald Heber, rev. by Charles P. Eden, 10 vols. (1847–1854), IV, 527. Elijah's cloud, which first appeared no larger than a man's hand but soon covered the sky (I Kings 18:44f.), was often used to illustrate the same idea: see the *Divine Meditations and Holy Contemplations* of Richard Sibbes, No. 318, in his *Complete Works*, edited by Alexander B. Grosart, 7 vols. (Edinburgh, 1862), VII, 224.

from seeming trifles, and the account of them in his autobiography may warn or encourage others, if the implication of each detail is made clear. Indeed, the more mundane the circumstances narrated, the more challenging the task of interpreting them spiritually.

This exercise gave authors and readers immense satisfaction. "How excellent and sweet an employment this is," declares one writer, "none can know, but those that have tasted it, and have the skill to spiritualize all objects, and providences, turning every thing by a Divine Chymistry, *in succum, sanguinem,* into spirit and nourishment." [28] John Livingstone, reflecting on the flourishing state of religion among Scottish Presbyterians in Ireland in the 1620's, says that "Some of them had attained such a dexterity of expressing religious purposes by the resemblance of worldly things, that being at feasts in common inns, where were ignorant profane persons, they would, among themselves, intertain spirituall discourse for ane long time; and the other professed, that although they spake good English, they could not understand what they said." [29]

[28] William Spurstow, *The Spiritual Chymist: Or, Six Decads of Divine Meditations on Several Subjects* (1666), Preface, sig. [A3ʳ]. Spurstow responds with great zest to the challenge of "improving" the mundane and trivial; his eighth Meditation, for instance, is "Upon a Crum going the wrong way" (pp. 11–12). On the value and necessity of "improving" natural objects, compare Ralph Austen, *The Spirituall use of an Orchard, or Garden of Fruit-Trees,* 2nd edition (Oxford, 1657), esp. the "Preface to the Reader," sigs. †2ʳ-[†4ᵛ]; cf. also Thomas Gouge, *The Young Man's Guide,* p. 116.

[29] "The Life of Mr. John Livingstone, Minister of the Gospell. Written by himself," in *Select Biographies,* I, 144. A piece by Isaac Watts entitled "Common Occurrences Moralized" shows that this habit of mind still thrived a century later, but that the "profane persons" were not always so acquiescent: see Watts's *Works,* 6 vols. (1810), IV, 606–07.

In the same vein, a Lancashire clergyman named John Machin had a singular ingenuity, as his biographer puts it, in improving every occurrence with unimaginable dexterity: "each Tree, and Bird, and Stone, would be a Text whereon he would aptly inlarge; having a mighty wit for the Spiritualizing of every thing, and gathering occasion of good Converse in every Company, and almost upon every matter." [30] Henry Newcome, who wrote Machin's life, shows typical admiration of this "mighty wit"; nor was he deficient in it himself, as his own diary reveals.[31]

Machin's ingenuity in spiritually "improving" ordinary objects and events extended to Biblical texts as well—to what Newcome calls "Scripture Similitudes." Imaginative exegesis enjoyed great popularity both in sermons,[32] where it often gave effective scope to the

[30] [Henry Newcome], *A Faithful Narrative of the Life and Death of That Holy and Laborious Preacher Mr. John Machin, Late of Astbury in the County of Chester* (1671), p. 61.

[31] *The Diary of the Rev. Henry Newcome, From September 30, 1661, to September 29, 1663,* edited by Thomas Heywood, Chetham Society *Remains,* Vol. xviii (Manchester, 1849). The survival of this "mighty wit" during the eighteenth century can be traced in a number of highly popular works, in addition to that of Isaac Watts already noted. See particularly the works of the Rev. James Hervey, which passed through numerous editions; for a charming specimen from the latter part of the century, cf. George Wright's *Walking Amusements for Chearful Christians, or Trades Spiritualized* (1775).

[32] See Rufus M. Jones, *Spiritual Reformers in the 16th and 17th Centuries* (1914), pp. 254–55. An anonymous contemporary of Defoe's flatly asserts that " 'tis obvious to every man in the least conversant with the Scriptures, that everywhere heavenly things are set forth by earthly representations; and that in great mercy and condescension to our capacities and understandings, and as helps to our faith": see *Christian Conversation, in Six Dialogues,* "iii. Between Eutocus and Fidelius, about Natural Things Spiritualized" (1840; 1st edition, 1720), pp. 10–11.

preacher's fancy, and in longer tracts, where it often enlivened and adorned otherwise dry arguments and precepts. A good instance is William Gurnal's *Christian in Compleat Armour* (1657), in which a single "Scripture Similitude"—the notable passage in the sixth chapter of Ephesians—is sufficiently elaborated to cover every aspect of Christian belief and conduct. St. Paul's description of the Christian soldier is, to be sure, a text whereon Gurnal could "aptly inlarge," yet the extent to which he did so is nevertheless remarkable. Others were similarly ambitious, though they seldom extrapolated entire treatises from single texts. A work entitled *Tropologia*, for example, undertakes to collect, compare, and explain the Biblical metaphors. The treatment of any single metaphor is almost perfunctory beside Gurnal's, but both books show how a general impulse toward "the Spiritualizing of every thing" could be brought to bear specifically on the Bible.[33] To the spiritually minded man, life and literature are equally rich in texts on which to enlarge; one could attach as much significance to a tradesman's annual inventory as to the Christian soldier's shield, helmet, and sword. Both life and literature are made up of similitudes, so that things seen and things read equally invite interpretation.

The wide currency of this outlook had two interesting results, both bearing on autobiography. In the first place, a number of Biblical people and things which were repeatedly subjected to this sort of interpretation took on well-defined spiritual values. Mere mention of

[33] B[enjamin] K[each] and T[homas] D[elaune], *Tropologia: A Key to open Scripture-Metaphors* (1682). The most relevant portions are Books II and III, by Keach, "Containing a Practical Improvement (Parallel-wise) of Several of the most Frequent and Useful Metaphors, Allegories, and Express Similitudes of the Old and New Testament."

them would suggest the spiritual import of whatever one happened to be describing. Since the process was perhaps too random and informal to be styled iconography, allusive shorthand might be a better term for it; in any case, it played an important role in spiritual autobiographies. Strange and uncommon experiences could be made familiar, singular and exotic episodes could be made meaningful, by even the most casual reference to Biblical precedents or analogues. Examples will be given later in the detailed discussion of actual autobiographies.

A second result of the tendency to regard everything in life and literature as amenable to spiritual interpretation was that certain ordinary objects and activities acquired distinct symbolic significance. Just as did certain Biblical objects and characters, so too a number of everyday articles and affairs took on definite spiritual connotations through constant figurative use. The two commonplace activities most frequently spiritualized have already been mentioned. From earliest times, preachers had described the Christian attitude toward this world and the next in terms of wayfaring. Although Protestant England left actual pilgrimages to Popish idolaters, one was still to reckon this earth "only as the land of our peregrination, and aspire after a better country." Bodily pilgrimage would no longer do, but spiritual pilgrimage was as necessary as ever. To exemplify and enforce it, preachers could now draw on the vivid details of overseas exploration and trade. Seafaring proved a rich field for those with a "singular ingenuity in improving every occurrence with unimaginable dexterity." [34]

[34] The popularity of nautical imagery in seventeenth-century preaching is indicated by an amusing passage on page 47 in [John Eachard], *The Grounds & Occasions of the Con-*

John Flavel, who had demonstrated his ability for such tasks in *Husbandry Spiritualized: Or, the Heavenly Use of Earthly Things*, published a work entitled *Navigation Spiritualized: Or, a New Compass for Seamen, Consisting of XXXII Points of Pleasant Observations, Profitable Applications, and Serious Reflections*. As a minister at Dartmouth in Devon, Flavel was in a good position to learn about sailors, ships, and the sea: he dedicates the work to the local "Masters Mariners and Seamen," who presumably supplied him with nautical lore and in return got his observations, applications, and reflections on it. There seem to have been few such systematic attempts to spiritualize navigation; Flavel asks that readers excuse defects in his effort, "wherein I find no precedent." [35]

---

tempt of the Clergy and Religion Enquired into (1670): "Metaphors, though very apt and allowable, are intelligible but to some sorts of Men, of this or that kind of Life, of this or that Profession: For example: Perhaps one Gentleman's metaphorical knack of Preaching comes of the Sea: And then we shall hear of nothing but *star-board* and *lar-board*, of *stems*, *sterns*, and *fore-castles*, and such like Salt-water Language: So that one had need take a Voyage to *Smyrna* or *Aleppo*, and very warily attend to all the Saylers Terms, before I shall in the least understand my Teacher. Now, although such a Sermon may possibly do some good in a *Coast-Town*, yet upward into the Countrey in an Inland-Parish, it will do no more than *Syriack* or *Arabick*."

[35] *Navigation Spiritualized*, in his *Whole Works*, II, 216. Two other works of the period probably resemble Flavel's, but I have seen neither: cf. W. Balmford, *Sea-man's Spiritual Companion, or Navigation Spiritualized. A Poem; being a new Compass for Seamen, consisting of Thirty-Two points, directing every Christian how to stear the Course of his Life through all Storms and Tempests* (1678); and *The Mariner's Divine Mate, or Spiritual Navigation improved in the right management of the Heavenly Voyage, by every one that intends to be saved: with serious Observations, and profitable Application* (1670). For a somewhat different view of this literature,

But one or another aspect of seafaring was often interpreted spiritually, as indeed one might expect in a maritime nation. "They that go down to the sea in ships, that do business in great waters" were constantly used to show "the works of the Lord, and his wonders in the deep" (Psalm 107:23).

Trade was the other activity whose mundane details were most frequently spiritualized. Just as seafaring tended to supplant overland pilgrimages in the imagery of peregrination, trade gradually overshadowed husbandry in the imagery of labor.[36] In the New Testament, of course, both commerce and agriculture furnish material for parables, and both continued to supply grounds for the pleasant observations, profitable applications, and serious reflections of men like Flavel. But the increasing importance of trade, and the

---

see R. H. Tawney, *Religion and The Rise of Capitalism* (N.Y., 1963), p. 201f.

[36] Husbandry did continue to furnish spiritual metaphors throughout the period. See the preface to "A Complete Account of the Life of Lieutenant Illidge," in Matthew Henry's *Miscellaneous Works* (1830), p. 1,106, where Illidge is called "an honest farmer, who was a good husband of his time, and was instructed by the grace of God how to cultivate his soul, as well as his ground, and suffer neither to be overgrown with briers and thorns."

Many contemporary works afforded the "honest farmer" guidance in the simultaneous cultivation of his soul and his ground: see Edward Welchman, *The Husbandman's Manual: Directing him how to improve the several actions of his Calling, and the most usual occurrences of his Life, to the glory of God, and the Benefit of his Soul* (1695). This manual had reached a twenty-fifth edition by 1818. Cf. also Edward Bury, *The Husbandman's Companion; containing one hundred occasional Meditations, Reflections, and Ejaculations, especially suited to men of that employment: directing them how they may be heavenly-minded, while about their ordinary Calling* (1677).

growing number of people engaged in it, made the merchant's routine and paraphernalia ever more inviting to preachers intent on showing the heavenly use of earthly things. Expanding commerce gave rise to new terms and techniques having obvious practical significance, yet demanding ingenious "improvement" to be brought within the pale of spiritually meaningful experience. Here indeed was occasion for "mighty wit" of the sort ascribed to John Machin: occasion, that is, for *discordia concors*, the discovery of occult resemblances in things apparently unlike. For Johnson's wry comment on the metaphysical poets can be applied with some justice to the spiritual metaphor-makers: "Of wit, thus defined, they have more than enough." [37] Seafaring and trade probably evoked more of this wit than other occupations, but nothing was exempt. Once spiritualized, all objects and activities were commensurable; one could assess their significance wherever he happened to encounter them, in books or personal experience. Needless to say, wit afforded no mere titillation in making this possible, since men's spiritual welfare was very much at stake.

2.

These assumptions about man's spiritual life not only affected the actual composition of autobiography, but gave the genre its double value, to writers and readers alike. A typical statement of the benefits to be derived from autobiography is advanced by Thomas Halyburton. He grants, modestly enough, that the common occurrences of the life of one "in all respects so inconsiderable" are not worth recording,

[37] *Lives of the English Poets*, edited by George Birkbeck Hill, 3 vols. (Oxford, 1905), 1, 20.

and insists that "it is none of my design to waste time or paper with these." But, he says, "if I can recount the Lord's gracious conduct towards me, and the state of matters both before and under the Lord's special dealings with me, in a way that shall tend to the conviction, illumination, conversion, consolation, and edification of the reader; and so arrange these topics as not only to illustrate the different parts of this work of grace, the several advances it made, the opposition made to it, its victory over this opposition of my own heart, of Satan and the world, but also to present the work in the several stages of its advancement, and in its final results; it may, at least, be of great use to my own confirmation." [38]

Whatever usefulness his autobiography may have for readers is seen by Halyburton as an extension of its primary value to himself. It was commonly felt that autobiography had this sequence of functions, the didactic growing out of the autodidactic. In any case, little stress was laid on the actual recording of experience, although this obviously had to precede any interpretations instructive to oneself or others. The consistent ability to get beyond the merely documentary, however, was one distinctive feature of spiritual autobiographies, and indeed of the diaries on which they were so often founded. Undertaken as a religious exercise, such compositions were not to dwell on the narration of fact: fact was to serve purely as ground for reflection, and allowing it to become an end in itself would be vain self-indulgence. Yet even the pious folk who did record their experiences in this spirit betray from time to time an unseemly relish for sheer narration, and supply more than that modicum

[38] *Memoirs*, p. 57.

of circumstantial detail required as a basis for "pleasant observations, profitable applications, and serious reflections." Even if the tale were introduced solely for the moral's sake, surprising pains might be taken in telling it. On one hand was the will to condense and curtail the factual record and to expatiate only on its spiritual significance; on the other, the propensity to expand a deserving narrative. One finds these conflicting tendencies in a considerable number of the diaries and autobiographies. The tension between them may explain in part the abruptness with which interpretation sometimes follows fact: the author, launching out in his account of something seen or done, will presently recall that only its spiritual implications really matter, and forthwith inserts them.

At any rate, it is an ability to see spiritual implications in experience of all sorts, rather than an account of overtly spiritual experience, that characterizes most of these diaries and autobiographies. What James Gordon kept, for instance, was not actually a spiritual diary, although much that he records has to do with men's souls. As a Scottish Episcopalian clergyman during a period of Presbyterian ascendancy, Gordon was preaching, pleading, and being persecuted: he had promising materials, in other words, for a spiritual diary. Yet he fails on the whole to "improve" these materials—fails to draw from them appropriate spiritual guidance or to weigh their significance for Scotland's spiritual welfare or his own. He generally confines himself to mere narration; the result is a very valuable picture of a clerical predicament similar in some respects to that of Swift at Kilroot, but it is not a spiritual diary.[39]

[39] *James Gordon's Diary 1692–1710*, edited by G. D. Henderson and H. H. Porter (Aberdeen, 1949).

The actual requirements and rewards of what I have called autodidacticism are well described by Oliver Heywood. One purpose of his autobiography, he declares, is "to inferre a good caution from the by-past for the remaining part of my life, that where I haue seen danger of a shipwreck I may obserue such rocks, and quicksands and charge mine owne hart with more jeolousy and watchfulnes, and make a covenant with my senses, members, facultys, and know satans devices, and where my strength and weaknes lyes: o what a helpful improuement may former experiences proue to future closewalking." [40] The Christian must pilot his soul with the alertness of a mariner: just as frequent soundings, diligently recorded, enable ships to avoid rocks and quicksands, so constant vigilance and reflection keep one clear of spiritual perils. A kindred analogy was used to illustrate autobiography's double instructiveness to author and reader. A ship's log is useful to him who keeps it and to others, should the voyage ever be repeated. Since every man is embarked on essentially the same spiritual journey, the record of one will be of use to all.[41]

Besides proving helpful to what Heywood calls "future closewalking," such a record can discipline and direct one's approach to recurrent events like birthdays, anniversaries, or the beginning of the new year, occasions on which a serious man like Heywood would renew his "covenant with my senses, members, facultys," or indeed draw up in form a new covenant with God. Certain holidays evoked similar reviews of past conduct and resolutions for the future, but the one

[40] *Autobiography*, p. 151.
[41] See John Ryther, *A Plat for Mariners: or, the Seamen's Preacher*, edited by S. Palmer (Cambridge, Mass., 1806; 1st edition, 1672), p. 55.

event that most frequently prompted the pious to written self-scrutiny was communion. In the memoir of his sister, Mrs. Radford, Matthew Henry speaks of "a constant register which she kept of all her approaches to the Lord's Supper." She began it at the age of seventeen, when she wrote as follows: "I was advised by my father to put these three questions to myself, for my help in preparation, and to examine myself upon them. What am I? What have I done? and what do I want? And by these three questions I did search and try myself, according to my weak ability, and what was amiss therein I humbly beg of God to pardon." [42]

A number of diaries consist largely of such "approaches to the Lord's Supper," and it is not surprising that their dominant tone should be confessional or penitential. Less obvious is the way this tone carries over into diaries not expressly concerned with preparations for communion. However frequently he might attend communion, a religious person would feel bound to "search and try" himself more often than he received the Sacrament.[43] Yet in the course of his

[42] Matthew Henry, *Memoirs*, pp. 318–19; for an interesting specimen of self-interrogation, see Section xxiv of John Shower's *Serious Reflections on Time and Eternity* (Glasgow, 1828; 1st edition, 1689), "Concerning the examination of a man's heart and life: the reasonableness, advantages, and necessity of it," especially paragraphs 1, 2, 7, and 8, pp. 149–50, 153–54.

[43] On frequency of communion, see Horton Davies, *Worship and Theology in England from Watts and Wesley to Maurice, 1690–1850* (Princeton, 1961), pp. 62–64. For other accounts of the methods and aims of searching and trying oneself, see Henry's preface to "A Concise Account of the Life of Lieutenant Illidge," in his *Miscellaneous Works*, p. 1,106; Lady Francis (Freke) Norton, *The Applause of Virtue* (1705), p. 108; [Abednego Seller], *The Devout Com-*

routine self-scrutiny, he might put to himself questions prescribed for the would-be communicant. As a result, self-assessment sometimes took the form of a prolonged or reiterated *mea culpa*. This phenomenon leads Arthur Ponsonby to assert of the religious diarists that they "do not show any real perspicacity in self-knowledge or self-analysis, because they generally take refuge in writing down more or less conventional religious formulae of self-disparagement." [44] But this critic, like the editor of Roger Lowe's diary discussed earlier, is unwarrantably harsh towards the conventional and formulaic. Again a taste for revealing idiosyncrasies is at odds with the aims of the diarists themselves, who regard with suspicion or abhorrence anything affecting to be novel or unique in matters of the spirit. Ponsonby also fails to note that self-congratulation is almost as frequent as self-disparagement: despair was as much to be avoided as complacency, and the question "What am I?" could elicit hopeful signs of grace as well as humiliating matter for repentance.

The crux of the matter, though, is that Mrs. Radford's "What am I?" was to be answered spiritually: if the responses were in a sense formulaic, this scarcely proves their lack of insight. The language of "heart anatomy" may have a more conventional ring than that of the psychologist, and its descriptive categories may be less flexible. But when the aim was to weigh the good and evil in one's actions, and to rejoice or repent

---

municant Exemplify'd In his behaviour Before, At, and After the Sacrament of the Lord's Supper, 9th edition (1704), pp. 38–44, "Strict Examination."

[44] *English Diaries: A Review of English Diaries from the Sixteenth to the Twentieth Centuries* (1923), p. 16.

accordingly, subtle explanation was out of place, and could actually prevent "real perspicacity": such was the conviction of the age, expressed with particular vehemence in the various condemnations of Jesuitical casuistry. However successful we may judge these diarists to have been in their efforts to attain self-knowledge, the fact remains that their real goal was self-instruction. The effectiveness of the cure might depend on the accuracy of the diagnosis, but it was the cure, not the diagnosis, that ultimately mattered.[45] To suppose otherwise is like quoting a half-verse dear to these diarists ("Let us search and try our ways") and then overlooking what they regarded as the crucial half ("and turn again to the Lord"—Lamentations 3:40).[46]

Self-instruction had as its goal a return to the Lord, as its method a search and trial of one's ways. The verse from Lamentations sums up the end and the means of autodidacticism, as found in the spiritual

[45] Compare the assertion of John Shower: "Remember that no man is the better merely for being examined, if there follows nothing after it. It is in order to a judgment to be passed upon ourselves. It is to search out our own iniquity, our beloved sin, in order to the mortification of it" (*Serious Reflections*, p. 155). Richard Lucas likewise observes that "the end of self-examination is not only to know your faults, but to mend them" (*The Plain Man's Guide to Heaven*, 3rd edition [1704], pp. 20–21). See also Thomas Ken on I Cor. 11:28, "Let a man examine himself, and so let him eat of that bread and drink of that cup," in his "Manual of Prayers for Winchester Scholars," in *Prose Works*, edited by William Benham (1889), pp. 221–27.

[46] On this text—and indeed for a comprehensive discussion of self-examination—see Edmund Arwaker, *Thoughts well Employ'd: Or, The duty of Self-Observation*, 2nd edition (1697), p. 76; cf. pp. 140–50 and *passim*. Defoe uses this text as the basis for an interesting dialogue on self-examination in *Due Preparations for the Plague*, pp. 145–47.

diaries and autobiographies. Little wonder that their composition was looked on as an act of piety; indeed, if one excepts praying and reading of the Bible, no act of private devotion was held in greater repute. The three exercises actually tended to be complementary, however, since the guidance sought from Scripture and the thanks or petitions offered in prayer were to be dictated on any given occasion by one's answers to "What am I?" and "What have I done?"

The record of one's experiments in self-searching and trial took on additional value as a pattern to others, since both the technique and its results were potentially edifying. As a consequence, many such records were kept or revised in presentable form for the sake of families, congregations, fellow-sufferers, or whatever group of readers the manuscript might reach, even by those who had no intention of publishing their lives to the world at large. Of all the diaries and autobiographies written, probably only a fraction were ever published; the majority were preserved and circulated in their original state if at all. But they did find their way into print in various forms.

In the first place, they were frequently incorporated in other works: funeral sermons, biographies, and works of practical divinity often contained autobiographical elements. These might be fragments inserted more or less in their native state, like the specimens of a diary given in Isaac Ambrose's *Media*. On the other hand, they might become integral parts of the work in which they occur. Donne's record of his illness in *Devotions upon Emergent Occasions* is a splendid example of autobiographical material essential yet subordinate to a work's main scheme; personal experience is assimilated into what is, in effect, an extended homily on the human condition. To be sure, autobiographical elements were seldom so fully transmuted into something universal and impersonal as in the *Devotions*. But works in traditional genres often drew on such material, sometimes merely for embellishment or illustration, but at times for their basic structure.

In the second place, some conventional types of literature incorporated autobiographical material to the extent that virtually new genres resulted. A curious specimen of this development is William Turner's *Compleat History of the Most Remarkable Providences, both of Judgment and Mercy, which have Hapned in this Present Age* (1697). In form it is clearly an outgrowth of a kind of encyclopedic history, organized thematically rather than chronologically, in which habits and deeds were gathered from widely different places and eras for didactic, apologetic, or polemic purposes.[47] Much of the work is in this vein, cataloguing or briefly recapitulating ancient and modern *exempla*. But it achieves some distinction through the constant use of autobiographical material, contributed by correspondents and inserted in the first person. As Vicar of Walberten in Sussex, Turner appears to have solicited information from clerical colleagues throughout the kingdom—a device whose journalistic possibilities had been explored earlier in the decade by John Dunton in the *Athenian Gazette*, so that it may be no mere coincidence that Dunton published this massive work. Nor does Turner actually claim great originality: his title-page describes the work as "set on Foot Thirty Years ago, by the Rever-

[47] Alan D. McKillop discusses Turner's compilation, and several others resembling it, in *The Early Masters of English Fiction* (Lawrence, 1956), pp. 11–12.

end Mr. Pool" and "since Undertaken and Finish'd" by himself. Nevertheless his blending of extracts from "the Best Writers" with the "Numerous Relations sent him from divers Parts of the Three Kingdoms" makes for a fresh, topical kind of history, and although the value of contributions from real or fictitious correspondents was grasped more quickly and fully by editors of periodicals, historians too became aware that first-person narrative afforded a desirable sense of reality and immediacy.[48] Turner himself neither invented the technique, nor exploited it fully, but his work does illustrate the effect autobiographical elements could have on traditional genres.

In any event, the tendency for autobiographies and diaries to be passed from hand to hand in manuscript was somewhat offset by their use in other types of literature, a phenomenon that must be taken into account in any survey of printed personal records. Such records had another kind of impact on literature, however, which was of far greater importance. By a process nearly the reverse of that just described, traditional types of literature could be cast in the form of autobiography. This was no mere matter of first-person rather than third-person narration. It involved a more basic sort of borrowing: the adoption of a distinctive way of organizing and interpreting experience. The new genre purporting to be autobiography imitated not only its voice but its shape and spirit. Its characteristic spirit, its manner of scrutinizing and "improving" everything seen, done, or thought, has

[48] Defoe himself was to exploit this technique several years later in *The Storm; Or, A Collection Of the most Remarkable Casualties and Disasters Which happen'd in the Late Dreadful Tempest, Both by Sea and Land* (1704).

already been suggested. But its typical shape—the larger structure into which it tended to mold narrative—remains to be described.

3.

The contents of spiritual autobiographies were naturally as diverse as the very lives of the men who wrote them. Nevertheless there was a strong tendency for such works to assume a regular, conventional shape. Before we analyze some autobiographies which exhibit this typical structure, it may be useful to suggest why there should have been a structure at all.

Organization of some kind is perhaps inevitable. Reviewing a span of time, an autobiographer must somehow make manageable and intelligible the sheer flux of events; he must find in it or foist upon it some minimal continuity or progression. Having to cope with the phenomenon of time is, in fact, his most elementary difference from the diarist. Whatever other points of divergence there may be, an autobiography will differ from a diary in having an element of pattern and direction, by means of which it resolves parcels of time into discrete periods or unfolding stages.

Various possibilities were open to the seventeenth-century biographer. A choice between imposed and natural patterns presented itself, although any ordering of experience is in a sense artificial and "imposed," yet at the same time "natural" insofar as it is a product or reflection of that experience. One imposed pattern, recognized as such but used nonetheless, was the division of one's past life into seven-year periods. This procedure had a certain "natural" foundation in the notion of the ages of man, and in the belief that one's body renews or replaces itself over a period of seven years.[49] But few men could claim that the significant developments in their lives fell into such convenient chronological periods. The appeal of this device, however, lay not so much in the tidiness it afforded one's narrative as in the way it facilitated a methodical casting up of spiritual accounts. The determination of one's total progress or decline in grace was after all a central function of such autobiography: the seven-year scheme, then, bridged the gap between a succession of miniature, interim self-trials and a final, comprehensive appraisal. By dividing the work into septennial chapters, one could sum up and perceive the drift of a whole series of daily, weekly, monthly, or annual self-assessments.

Another pattern sometimes imposed on spiritual autobiography was a chapter division according to changes of occupation or status. As far as the narrative was concerned, this device was less arbitrary than the seven-year division. But it proved rather inadequate as a framework for spiritual autobiography since it shared the basic drawback of the septennial scheme:

[49] These beliefs probably originated in antiquity, but continued to find adherents throughout this period. Sir Thomas Browne observes that "the daies of men are cast up by Septenaries, and every seventh year conceived to carry some altering character with it, either in the temper of body, minde, or both" (*Pseudodoxia Epidemica*, Book IV, Ch. xii, 2nd edition [1650], p. 177). Cf. Jeremy Taylor, *The Rule and Exercises of Holy Dying*, Ch. I, Sect. I, in *Works*, III, 267. For an interesting specimen of spiritual autobiography organized by septenaries, see *The Life of Adam Martindale* [1624–1686], *Written by Himself*, edited by Richard Parkinson, Chetham Society *Remains*, Vol. IV (Manchester, 1845).

the stages of a man's spiritual development seldom coincide with changes in his worldly situation any more than with fixed periods of time.

There was, however, a "natural" pattern available. Preceding sections have shown how these autobiographies found significance in all sorts of actions and situations by regarding them in a spiritual context. Careers that were totally unlike in their outward character turned out to be basically similar when viewed in this way, since "the work of the Lord, in substance, is uniform and the same in all," and "God's Dealings are much what the same with all his Servants in the main." However diverse their outward lives, all Christians shared the same spiritual purpose and plight; nor was their likeness confined to a vague overall indentity of predicament. More specifically, their souls underwent identical stages of development: between one spiritual pilgrimage and another, the course of successes and setbacks varied considerably in intensity but remarkably little in sequence. Spiritual striving (and for that matter spiritual decay as well) seemed to obey a pattern of its own. The stages composing this pattern were at once temporal and thematic; their progression was regular and determinate. Every man at every juncture could place himself, if he took the trouble, in a recognizable phase of spiritual development. Further general description of this pattern will be less helpful than an analysis of its actual components. Enough has been said, however, to suggest the grounds of its appeal as a structural device. It did seem to render faithfully the innate contours of spiritual development; and since such development obeys no calendar, and seldom tallies with changes in one's outward affairs, neither the scheme of seven-year epochs nor the arrangement based on shifts in station proved serviceable.

What actually came to be the dominant shape of spiritual autobiography can be seen clearly in the memoirs of James Fraser of Brae, written around 1670. Fraser was then in his thirties, living rather precariously on a legally entangled, debt-encumbered inheritance; he was soon to enter the Presbyterian ministry, fully aware that he was doing so at a most inauspicious time. Born into a family of some substance and note, soundly educated, distrustful of rhapsodic religious fervor, he was socially and temperamentally remote from the "mechanick preachers" whom William York Tindall has brought to light, the strident sectaries whose self-advertisements stand in the background of *Grace Abounding* (see page x above). Fraser's memoirs merit attention partly for this very reason; they demonstrate that spiritual autobiography was not the exclusive domain of narrow fanatics and canting enthusiasts. Fraser's zeal is moderated by a sense of decorum. He does not strain to appear monstrously sinful before conversion, or exceptionally sanctified afterward: glorifying God, he does not covertly glorify himself. The lyrical ejaculations of men like Bunyan are deservedly well known. Less familiar, however, are the writings of men like Fraser who allow themselves no such license. Such works exist in considerable numbers, none the less pious for being somewhat guarded, their authors none the less devout for being gentlemen.

The structure of Fraser's memoirs is actually quite simple. "I shall reduce what I have met with," he says in the Preface, "to these eight heads":

"(1). What hath been the Lord's carriage to me before I knew any thing of God, or had so much as the form of religion. (2.) Some steps of God's providence while the Lord was drawing me to himself; or some preparation-work to my conversion, while my heart was not fully changed, but had only some appearance of godliness. (3.) Some things concerning my conversion, the time and manner; and what immediately followed. (4.) Of the sad and long decay that happened thereafter. (5.) Relate some things touching my recovery out of that decay. (6.) Some things that happened immediately after this recovery, for the space of four or five years. (7.) Some things relating to my present condition, and some things I have observed in my experience. (8.) Some particular mercies I have met with from the Lord at several occasions." [50]

Within this framework a still more elementary pattern is discernible. Conversion is clearly the pivotal phase in the sequence; apart from the eighth heading, which stands outside the sequence to recount one facet of it, each stage not only precedes or follows conversion in point of time, but takes on significance wholly as a preparation or obstacle to it beforehand, or as a result or retrogression from it once achieved.

Everything is seen as happening before, during, or after conversion, yet there is room in such a scheme for considerable variation and complexity. [51] The natural

[50] "Memoirs of the Rev. James Fraser of Brae, Minister of the Gospel at Culross. Written by Himself," in *Select Biographies*, II, 87.

[51] On this matter see Roger Sharrock's valuable introduction to *Grace Abounding* (Oxford, 1962), pp. xxix-xxxi; cf. also J. H. Taylor, "Some Seventeenth-Century Testimonies," in *Transactions* of the Congregational Historical Society, XVI (1949), p. 66.

man might pass through various kinds and degrees of sinfulness, and the regenerate man was by no means immune from or invulnerable to Satan's further assaults. The actual process of conversion, moreover, differed for every man in occasion, duration, and intensity. Fraser's own quiet deliberateness enables him to give a particularly good picture of developments leading up to and following his conversion. Even in describing the conversion itself he is analytical, not agitated; reflective, not rapturous.

Fraser's account of his childhood is quite perfunctory. Looking back on the period before he "knew any thing of God, or had so much as the form of religion," Fraser gives only the barest sketch. He does mention, however, his sullen disposition and peevish temper: froward and unruly, his very infancy made evident the necessity of regeneration and the fact that "by nature we are under the power of sin and Satan" (pp. 89–90). Before long he mastered the forms and externals of religion, yet he remained as much in his sorry natural state as before: natural, that is, in the Pauline sense: "the natural man receiveth not the things of the Spirit of God . . . neither can he know them, because they are spiritually discerned" (I Corinthians 2:14). To languish in this state of nature, one obviously need not be an ignorant savage, since a man well versed in religious matters may remain a hopeless Pharisee. Young as he was, Fraser soon developed a lifeless, legalistic spirit; the business of religion amounted to no more than a dry formalism. Yet one gets few glimpses of actual transgressions, which in any case were too mild and infrequent to earn him any Bunyanesque title to having been the chief of sinners. In fact, his youthful essays in wickedness were never really successful; all were thwarted by the same force that prompted them: the vigilance and sternness of school discipline. Even in retrospect he takes a graver view of these little sallies than one would today. He does not exaggerate the wickedness of any single action, but finds them collectively symptomatic of an innate tendency to wickedness. He does not pretend to have been unnaturally depraved, just naturally depraved.

The period preceding Fraser's conversion extends up through his seventeenth or eighteenth year, and except for the final year or two, when he was at college, his outward behavior had little about it to suggest that he was undergoing "preparation-work to conversion." His growing self-awareness, for instance, fell far short of repentance. "I had in the meantime," he says, "some sharp and terrible convictions for particular sins, but not for my evil nature . . . I mourned for sin, not because it offended God, but because of the consequents of it" (pp. 102–03). This attitude may be contrasted with a contemporary definition of repentance as "a hearty Sorrow for your Sins already past, and solemn, serious Resolutions, to commit no more; and this Sorrow must proceed not only from a Fear of eternal Punishment, but from a Hatred of Sin, for its own evil Nature, and as it is offensive to the Holiness of God." [52] So Fraser was still among those who, as he puts it, "profess, and yet sin on still; that fear the Lord, and serve their idols" (p. 97).

In any case, his spiritual progress was by no means steady or uninterrupted. Some episodes brought him nearer conversion, others put it off; nor does he at-

[52] Daniel Defoe, *The Family Instructor*, 2 vols. (1756), I, 188.

tempt to conceal these fluctuations. What he does is to weigh each in terms of its effect on his conversion, either as advancing or retarding it: they have a constant focus, but not a consistent trend. Seldom, in fact, was there a gradual transition from a natural to a regenerate state. In most spiritual autobiographies, the crucial stage is rather abrupt, however much "preparation-work" may precede it. A man could wallow more and more deeply in his natural state, reaching complete degeneration through a gradual process of hardening in villainy, but progress in the opposite direction followed no such unbroken sequence. Between the best of natural men and the least of the regenerate there was a wide gap, since the grace necessary to conversion had to come ultimately as God's gift, not as one's own attainment.

Although the total structure of a narrative like Fraser's thus appears fairly simple and unified, this orderliness does not extend to individual incidents. Events more or less explicitly related to the central theme of conversion often seem to have little relation to one another. Between two successive episodes, in other words, a direct, causal connection may be altogether lacking; nevertheless they will be significantly related by virtue of having a common point of reference, the conversion which each either hastens or delays.

In spite of being the crux of the entire narrative, Fraser's account of his actual conversion occupies only three pages out of more than two hundred. One reason seems to be the desire to avoid any imputation of enthusiasm; another, the task of reconciling the genuineness of this rebirth with all the backslidings that follow. At all events, the account is not so condensed that it omits the classic features of conversion. For instance, the turning-point is usually preceded by despondency. Whether or not there has been a long course of prior preparation, there is usually a climax of physical or mental agony and an overpowering sense of helplessness or abandonment immediately before conversion. Fraser's brief account conforms to this pattern: "discouragements did quite overwhelm me, and fears of drawing on more guilt did load me; and, withal, this apprehension lay heavy on me, and haunted me like a ghost, That it was in God's mind never to do me good; so that fear, discouragement, vexation, and despair, and some horror and grief, did all take hold of me. . . . Hanging, therefore, by this small thread, I went to prayer with many sad complaints; and the Lord, while I was like the prodigal son yet a great way off, ran to meet me" (pp. 110–11). As is typical of such narratives, Fraser's own share in his conversion is no greater or more meritorious than the prodigal's in his return: in each case the credit is due solely to the father, who spontaneously reclaims and restores the wretched son. Again, it has been mentioned that in most of these narratives the conversion, when it finally occurs, is somewhat abrupt; in this, too, Fraser's experience is typical. The change, such as it is, is instantaneous.[53]

Fraser's account of conversion differs from many others in its restraint. Despite its brevity, no essential ingredients are omitted: what has been left out is the

[53] One should perhaps emphasize that it is conversion, not total regeneration, that occurs abruptly. The distinction will be elaborated in later chapters, but see Joseph Hall, *The Second Century of Meditations and Vows*, No. LXXVIII, in his *Works*, VII, 475–76; cf. also Obadiah Sedgwick, *The Parable of the Prodigal* (1660), pp. 88–89.

usual description of the indescribable joy of casting off
the old man and becoming a new. In its place one finds
such terse statements as the following: "I thought
now, no Scriptures for me but such as were directed to
saints, and therefore read some chapters of the Second
Epistle of Peter, but found little life. This did shake
me" (p. 112).[54] Fraser is not altogether cold and
unmoved, but he is not carried away by the heady
elation of being reborn. The cause may be his wariness
of seeming an enthusiast, but the problem of accounting for later relapses seems to be more relevant. The
same day Fraser experiences conversion, he finds his
sense of triumph and assurance ebbing. In fact, he no
sooner finds "all the clouds evanished which were
betwixt the Lord and my soul," than new clouds
appear on the horizon. Although he observes that
"now I was persuaded that I was converted, and was
come to that pitch which formerly I wanted [i.e.
lacked]," he goes on to say that "this continued in its

[54] Fraser's tone should be contrasted with that of a typical
Ranter. What follows, for instance, is Joseph Salmon's description of his "great experience": "Time would faile to tell
what joy unspeakable, peace inconceivable, what soul-ravish-
ing delights, and most divinely infatuating pleasures my soul
was here possest with. I could cast my eye no where but that
presence of love presented itselfe to me whose beatificall
vision at times dazzled me into a sweet astonishment. In a
word, I can give you no more perfect account of that glory
which then covered me; the lisps and slipps of my tongue will
but render that imperfect, whose pure perfection surmounts
the reach of the most strenuous and high-flown expression. I
appeared to myselfe as one confounded into the abyss of
eternitie, nonentitized into the being of beings, my soul spilt
and emptied into the fountaine and ocean of divine fulness,
expired into the aspires of pure life." (Quoted in Rufus M.
Jones, *Studies in Mystical Religion* [1909], p. 476, from
Salmon's work of 1651, *Heights in Depths, and Depths in
Heights*.)

strength only for a quarter of an hour, and then it abated as to its measure, though not altogether; but something remained." [55]

Conversion, then, brings no immunity to further spiritual vicissitudes, but it does supply a new orientation from which to face them, and a new strength with which to endure or overcome them.[56] Although events following conversion occur over a period of time no longer than that preceding conversion, they occupy considerably more space in Fraser's narrative. It is not that they are more clearly recalled for being recent, or that they are regarded as intrinsically more important for being the experiences of maturity. It has to do instead with the overall function of his memoirs—to edify rather than merely record. Those who were saved late in life, or after a full-blown career in sin, seldom had to go beyond their conversions for instructive or monitory material. But those who had only a normal share of youthful excesses to their account, and who experienced conversion before they had hardened in desperate sins, obviously had to look to a later period for edifying matter. It can be stated almost as a law of spiritual autobiographies that the greater the attention paid to events before conversion, the less emphasis given to what happens afterwards, and vice versa. A

[55] *Ibid.*; cf. Obadiah Grew's *Meditations upon our Saviour's Parable of the Prodigal Son* (1678), p. 19.

[56] Looking back on his conversion, Fraser observes that "ever thereafter, although there have been tentations, and shakings, and interruptions, yet hath that spunk never died which was kindled, but hath been growing at last, more and more; some good ever remained, and in my sorest decays, the impressions of God's dealing at this time remained, . . . which was the means to reduce me out of a backsliding condition" (p. 120). Compare Edward Waple, *Thirty Sermons Preached on Several Occasions* (1714), pp. 397–98.

work that traces in detail the progress of sin, with conversion finally snatching the author from the very jaws of hell, will rarely have much to say about subsequent relapses. But where the author's fortunate environment or precocious piety has preserved him from great wickedness before conversion, the trials to which he is later exposed usually furnish the required exemplary matter.

Fraser is clearly in this latter category. His conversion, far from ending his spiritual turmoils, opens the way to many which his Pharisaical complacency had kept from breaking out previously. He is now forced to cope with impulses which conversion itself cannot eradicate, but rather brings painfully to the surface. For there is not, as one divine points out, "such a subjection in the will of a regenerate man, as to make *no resistance* to the *commands* or *disposals* of almighty God: for then there would never be any of those *struggles,* or *conflicts,* which good men continually complain of, between *grace* and *corruption:* but there is such a subjection in him that is *born again*, that, in his *esteem*, he gives a *preference* to the will of God; and, in his *endeavours*, strives to be more and more conformed to it; and, in *fact*, this does at last *prevail* against all the *enslaving* motions of an untoward volition and inclination." [57]

Here the latter portion of Fraser's memoirs is virtually summarized. He has his full share of struggles between grace and corruption, and although "the en-

[57] Samuel Wright, *A Treatise on That Being Born Again Without Which No Man Can Be Saved* (N.Y., 1813), pp. 121–22. Wright's "Recommendatory Letter" was published with Defoe's *Family Instructor* in the same year that this *Treatise* first appeared (1715).

slaving motions of an untoward volition and inclination" are not, in the long run, allowed to have the best of it, they do win a number of minor sieges and skirmishes. These internal campaigns need not be recounted: their aggregate effect is to carry on and consolidate the work of grace begun by conversion. Like a successful general, Fraser is careful to detail the strategy and maneuvers that should bring victory to his readers in their own battles. In saying as he does that "I have in nothing been more refreshed, quickened, and edified, than by hearing and reading of the spiritual experiences of others" (p. 85), he serves notice that readers must in turn apply and improve what he has written.

By the same token, a prominent feature of these sections of Fraser's memoirs is a record of his own reading. The inclusion in such narratives of what were in effect bibliographies was a common practice, clearly in keeping with the habit of diagnosing one's own spiritual condition by comparing it with the case histories of others. These references varied in extent from one work to another: sometimes they were limited to occasional allusions to the Bible, but often they amounted to regular catalogues of choice divinity. At any rate, the incorporation of such material in autobiographies was another factor that contributed to their highly conventional quality.

Fraser's memoirs deal at some length, then, with his struggle to retain and extend the effects of conversion, but one finds the impetus to this spiritual exertion coming as often from things read as from things done. As a result, the emphasis shifts still further towards contemplation. It is not merely that the narrative is punctuated with constant analysis and reflection: the

narrative itself becomes largely a record of analyses
and reflections. Instead of keeping pace with his actions, the process of self-examination tends to become
an independent activity. Fraser himself seems to have
been aware of this, however, and has an interesting
comment on it: "Satan, by making me pore excessively
on evidences of grace, and by occupying me in laying
continually the foundation and trying it, as thinking it
never sure enough, hath thereby kept me from my
generation-work, and from progress in grace; in which
exercises, if I had been as diligent as in examination of
myself, I might have been assured more quickly, 2 Pet.
1:10. It is true, we should examine our states, 2 Cor.
13:5, but it is wrong to be only and continually taken
up with this" (p. 293). From Fraser's point of view, of
course, this is a spiritual dilemma; he is not concerned
with its aesthetic implications. Yet a preoccupation
with self-scrutiny certainly affects the literary quality
of his memoirs. Spiritual autobiography requires, almost by definition, considerable poring on evidences
of grace: the problem is one of degree, since either too
much or too little can spoil the work. If there is too
little, the events narrated lose their significance as
tokens of spiritual soundness or illness; moreover, scat-
tered attempts to give them such significance will
appear contrived and extraneous, if not insincere. On
the other hand, an autobiography runs hazards in
dwelling too much on self-scrutiny. If the sketchiest of
narratives is forced to sustain ponderous spiritualiza-
tions, the outlines of the author's own personality tend
to be obliterated and his life reduced to a series of
abstractions. The narrative must submit to organizing
principles, but narrative there must be: spiritual
themes have to control the narrative without unduly

confining or, as occasionally happens, virtually supplanting it.

Exactly how much narrative and spiritualization make a well-balanced spiritual autobiography may be impossible to specify. Nevertheless the presence of each in proportion is perhaps the most basic criterion of literary merit that one can apply. To be sure, the spiritual autobiographer himself seldom appears to strive for this balance; his procedure, however conscious and calculated in some respects, is dictated by no such belletristic norms. Yet there does seem to have been an implicit awareness that narrative and spiritualization must go hand in hand, a realization that neither can utterly outstrip the other if the work is to be both interesting and edifying. In time, with the rise of fiction purporting to be autobiography, the desirability of this balance came to be explicitly recognized and asserted. The prefaces to such works were to boast almost invariably that a faithful narrative had been judiciously interspersed with serious reflections, and that the observations and precepts lent point to the narrative while deriving from it in return their exemplary force. This, at any rate, is what the prefaces would claim; what actually happened to this nicely balanced reciprocity will be seen in later chapters, when fictitious autobiographies are discussed in detail. Before we discuss works clearly in this category, however, it will be useful to examine a book which illustrates the transition from genuine to feigned spiritual memoirs; thereby the conventional shape of all such memoirs can be further elaborated.

CHAPTER II

The Transition to Fiction

In 1708 there appeared a book entitled, *An Account of Some Remarkable Passages in the Life of a Private Gentleman; with Reflections thereon. In Three Parts: Relating to Trouble of Mind, some violent Temptations, and a Recovery; in order to awaken the Presumptuous, and encourage the Despondent.* The title of another issue the same year adds a third function (*to convince the Sceptick*) and describes the anonymous work as *Left under his own hand, to be communicated to the Publick after his Decease.* This ample prospectus introduces an octavo volume of some three hundred pages; a second edition, "with Additions from the Author's Original Papers," was issued in 1711.[1]

Like many anonymous works of the period, this one has been linked at times with the name of Defoe; it is given him by Esdaile and by Halkett and Laing, though not by Trent or Moore.[2] For purposes of this

[1] All subsequent references are to the 1711 edition. A further edition—apparently an abridgment—is mentioned by William H. McBurney in his *Check List of English Prose Fiction 1700–1739* (Cambridge, Mass., 1960): No. 31b, *An Abstract of the Remarkable Passages In the Life of a Private Gentleman* (1715).

[2] Arundell Esdaile, *English Tales and Romances from 1475 to 1740* (1912), p. 201; Samuel Halkett and John Laing, *Dictionary of Anonymous and Pseudonymous English Literature*, 4 vols. (1882–1888), I, 13. William P. Trent, bibliography of Defoe in *The Cambridge History of English Literature*,

study, however, it matters little who the author was. The preceding chapter has sketched the general character of late seventeenth- and early eighteenth-century spiritual autobiography: it remains to describe the evolution from genuine memoirs towards the kind of fiction Defoe was to write, and the *Account* merits attention because it represents an intermediate stage in this process. It would be very convenient to my argument, of course, to be able to show Defoe using materials or techniques that could have come only from the *Account*, and even more opportune to be able to demonstrate that it was his own early work. The fact that I can do neither, however, in no way lessens the book's usefulness as an illustration of certain conventional elements of spiritual autobiography persisting alongside newer features typical of the fiction to come.[3]

---

edited by A. W. Ward and A. R. Waller, 14 vols. (N.Y., 1907–1917), IX, 466–82; John Robert Moore, *A Checklist of the Writings of Daniel Defoe* (Bloomington, 1960). Over a century ago Walter Wilson declared that "whether De Foe had any share in handing these papers to the world, may be questioned, as there is nothing but common report to warrant the supposition" (*Memoirs of the Life and Times of Daniel De Foe*, 3 vols. [1830], III, 29). The four works just cited offer no evidence to confirm or refute Wilson's assertion.

[3] There are various indications that the *Account* is not a genuine autobiography. It purports to be a physician's recital of his own experiences, but compared with such a work as Sir Thomas Browne's *Religio Medici*, there is little that is distinctively medical in its subject matter or general outlook. What few medical references there are deal mainly with melancholy—an ailment that fascinated physicians and laymen alike (see n. 14 below)—and look suspiciously as though they were garnered from Burton's *Anatomy* or some similar compendium. And at one point a statement begins with the words, "Physicians say . . . ," as if the author had forgotten momentarily that he is one himself (p. 105).

One can best illustrate its transitional character by proceeding at once to analyze its contents. The first part of the *Account* is rather barren of "Remarkable Passages," largely because the Private Gentleman's early environment is wholesome and respectable, like that of Fraser before and Crusoe after him. Without describing it at all precisely, or affording any homely, familiar details, he establishes that there was no lack of provision for either his worldly or spiritual welfare. But in none of these cases can favorable circumstances shield the young man against evil within himself, against his own innate impulse to folly and wickedness. In Fraser this natural tendency to evil is present, but finds no very dramatic outlets; in Crusoe it issues forth as radical disobedience. It likewise besets the young Private Gentleman. The resulting misdeeds are not always specified, yet there emerges a pattern of deepening guilt which closely resembles that of Crusoe. Both embark on wayward careers through initial gestures of rebellion: Crusoe defies his father by running off to sea, and although no single action of the Private Gentleman so drastically flouts paternal authority, he eventually perceives that his sufferings have been in part the punishment, and in part the direct consequence, of his early breach of duty. As he puts it, "I smarted the more, I'm confident, for the neglect of paternal Advice; let the Rebellious consider it, and

---

Furthermore, the chronology of the author's early reading belies his assumed age. To demonstrate this in detail would be tedious. It is enough to point out that in 1708 the author, after a long and responsible career, is lately deceased; yet he could not have been born before 1660, for he claims to have read as a child a book that first appeared in 1671 (pp. 2–3), and to have read as a young man one book that came out in 1696, and another first published in 1692 (p. 44).

know assuredly, God may be a slow, but will be a sure Avenger of any Degrees of such unnatural Contempt" (pp. 134–35). Rather than acquiesce in his proper role, and accept his station in the social and moral order, each young man acts the prodigal, Crusoe by actually absconding, the Private Gentleman by pursuing a headstrong, unruly course at home. Once repudiated, environment and training come to lose their influence: willful and heedless, both young men reach the state of those who, as the Private Gentleman expresses it, "wear out the Force of their Education, till it becomes a Curse to them, rendring their Guilt more notorious" (p. 7). In the process, each shows clear symptoms of his gradually worsening condition.

The Private Gentleman's first outward sign of spiritual degeneration is his disregard of Providential occurrences. As mentioned earlier, a constant theme of the spiritual diaries and autobiographies is that prudence and thankfulness alike oblige one to be attentive and responsive to the workings of Providence. Since God intends them to warn, instruct, or encourage, the failure to heed them is both rash and undutiful.[4] But crises which ought to bring the Private Gentleman to submission and repentance make only fleeting impres-

---

[4] Indeed, it reduces a man to the level of beasts: see Isaac Barrow, "On the Gunpowder Treason," in *Theological Works*, edited by Alexander Napier, 9 vols. (Cambridge, 1859), I, 448–49. Cf. Joseph Hall, *Soliloquies: Or, Holy Self-Conferences of the Devout Soul, upon sundry choice occasions*, No. VII, "Trust upon Trial," in *Works*, edited by Philip Wynter, 10 vols. (Oxford, 1863), VIII, 28. In the same vein, the Private Gentleman finds that he has some symptoms of the plague, which, as he recalls, "struck me into a mighty Consternation; but, alas! God removing speedily the Danger, Security crept upon me. I look'd to Second Causes; too little to the Hand that threaten'd or deliver'd; like a stupid Wretch, unaffected with Frowns or Kindnesses" (p. 12).

sions on him: "I Travell'd now abroad, where I escaped many Dangers; and in my Passage home, a very remarkable one: In the midst of the Storm, I form'd a Resolution, ne'er to forget the Mercy, if God would spare me; but I soon basely forgot it, and ne'er solemnly remember'd it, till God awaken'd me by his Judgments" (p. 16). Like Crusoe in his first storm at sea, he does initially recognize such terrifying events as expressions of God's wrath; he cannot "wear out the Force of [his] Education" all at once. But by lapsing into security as soon as such dangers pass, and by failing to keep resolutions made under stress, both Crusoe and the Private Gentleman become hardened to Providential chastisements and deliverances. At first they are merely recalcitrant, but gradually they come to be oblivious. "God often flash'd Terrors in my Face, in his Providential Dealings, but I saw not his Hand," admits the Private Gentleman (p. 7), and Crusoe's vicissitudes are marked by the same obtuseness, as will be shown in detail later.

One symptom of the Private Gentleman's spiritual decay, then, is his casting off superior rule and guidance, whether paternal or divine. This fundamental error leads to further missteps. In the spiritual autobiographies, actions or attitudes that put off conversion are represented in terms of withdrawal from God: in the *Account* this process of estrangement is made quite vivid, although it was to be described still more effectively in *Robinson Crusoe*. In neither book does the hero become entirely alienated from God, for it proves impossible to escape omnipresence.[5] Nevertheless both works manage to suggest spiritual disaffection through

[5] On this point see Obadiah Grew, *Meditations upon our Saviour's Parable of the Prodigal Son* (1678), pp. 119–20, and Obadiah Sedgwick, *The Parable of The Prodigal* (1660), p. 8.

the language of physical distance, and indicate through bodily wanderings that the hero is spiritually astray. Both Crusoe and the Private Gentleman reenact the error of the Prodigal Son, learning only through bitter experience that "While you run out of God's Way," as the *Account* puts it, "you flie the only Center of Rest and Safety" (p. 13). Crusoe's vagrancy is described more fully than the Private Gentleman's, but is essentially the same; the only difference is that Crusoe acts out on three continents a process that the Private Gentleman goes through at home. One might infer from the following passage that the Private Gentleman's peregrinations rivalled those of Crusoe himself: "Like a Sick Man that tumbles for Ease by change of Posture, I roll'd from one Vanity to another, but still carried with me my Distemper: God hedg'd up my Way thus, to reduce me from my Wandrings, and I, instead of Compliance, was striving to find new By-Paths to run from him: The Center of Rest offer'd to be my Repose, but I still followed my own Inventions." [6] But in fact he seems to have ventured abroad only once: all this imagery of fitful, agitated motion has to do with his spiritual state, not his overt deeds. Without literally wasting his substance in a far country, the Private Gentleman behaves like the prodigal, as indeed every unregenerate man must. For as

---

[6] *Account*, p. 24. In *The Vanity of the World* (1658), Ezekiel Hopkins adapts and elaborates the metaphor of the sick man from Plutarch (*Works* [1701], p. 18). The rest of the passage is equally conventional; cf. Sedgwick, *Parable of the Prodigal*, p. 237: "Every lost man is in a false way, in a by-way; his ways are sinful ways: The lost man, he is out of the common and known Road; he is in the Woods, in the Ditches, in the Deserts, in the Fields, and he goes from one strange place to another strange place."

one divine explains, "Man naturally loves changes of states and conditions, as feaverish palates do change of beer, and it may be none will please. . . . It may in some sort be said of every natural mans heart, as of *Nebuchadnezzars, a beasts heart was given unto him* (Dan. 4:16). Man would have change of pasture, as some beasts will not stay where they are put, but break and leap Hedges to get into new grounds. Not only many of the Angels *left their first estate* (Jude 6), but all men in the first man left theirs; Man still wants something." [7]

The Private Gentleman's own attempts to evade responsibility and escape painful self-awareness actually lead him no further afield than the playhouse and other local haunts of idleness and dissipation. Yet such action differs from Crusoe's only in geographical scope, not in spiritual implication. Crusoe does essentially the same thing in a more extended, more palpable way. The spatial imagery of flight from God is perhaps more appropriate to Crusoe's forlorn far-flung rambles than to domestic "changes of Posture," but it affords the Private Gentleman a graphic analogy for a kind of inward experience that would be hard to describe directly. By means of it, at any rate, he does manage to convey his spiritual predicament, as in the following passage: "I thought to get rid of my Fears and Fansies, by running from God; which was only to be effected by running to Him; a most fatal and common Error. . . . Let that vain Man know, whoever he be, that takes any Method like this, to stifle or divert the Rebukes of his Conscience: Let him know, I say, that the Issue will be, that either his

[7] Grew, *Meditations*, p. 48; cf. Sedgwick, *Parable of the Prodigal*, p. 236.

Horrors will multiply upon him, or what is infinitely worse, and indeed the worst that can befal him in this World, God will give him up to hardness of Heart" (p. 40). Stiff-necked resistance may stir God to greater severity; on the other hand, it may provoke him to abandon the obdurate man to his own ruin. Flight is most disastrous precisely when it appears to have succeeded, for as the Private Gentleman points out, "Let such as run to their little shifts in Distress, consider, if they prosper, 'tis a Curse: If God design them good, he'll ne'er leave them till he has whipp'd them home from their Idols, as a tender Father does refractory Children, till he sufficiently humble them." [8] Thus the condition of men who forsake God is not hopeless until he in turn forsakes them. It is really desperate, not when God hinders or chastises them, but when he forbears, leaving them to sin on in security. Neither Crusoe nor the Private Gentleman ever reaches this final stage; shift and dodge as they will, God stays in pursuit. But both arrive at such a pitch of hardness that only the most drastic methods can bring them to submission. The graver their mal-

[8] *Account*, p. 114. Cf. Hopkins, *Works*, p. 19; William Payne, *A Practical Discourse of Repentance* (1695), pp. 287–88; and Hebrews 12: 6–11. Jeremy Taylor sums up the matter in "The Mercy of the Divine Judgments," *Works*, edited by Reginald Heber, rev. by Charles P. Eden, 10 vols. (1847–1854), IV, 487: "if God suffers men to go on in sin and punishes them not, it is not a mercy, it is not a forbearance; it is a hardening them, a consigning them to ruin and reprobation: and themselves give the best argument to prove it; for they continue in their sin, they multiply their iniquity, and every day grow more enemy to God; and that is no mercy that increases their hostility and enmity with God. A prosperous iniquity is the most unprosperous condition in the whole world."

ady, the harsher the medicine God must administer; as the Private Gentleman reflects afterwards, "Any that observe the various Passages of my Life past, will plainly perceive a Gradation of Sins and Judgments, which center'd finally in a desperate Complication of Sin and Misery, with the utmost Danger of what was infinitely worse" (p. 133).

At one point, indeed, he concludes that he is a "castaway." But in saying this, he supposes himself beyond assistance, not beyond punishment, for as he also observes, there is "no refuge for a Soul pursued with Storms of Divine Wrath" (pp. 93–94, 97). It is needless to insist on the similarity of Crusoe's situation; here again the Private Gentleman is describing figuratively a process which Crusoe undergoes bodily. When the Private Gentleman pictures himself as a castaway, or God's wrath as the storm that overwhelms him, he does no more than express his spiritual plight in lively but conventional terms: [9] tempest and shipwreck are metaphors for ordeals purely within himself. In Crusoe's case, however, they are elements in the outward as well as the inward action; narrative and spiritual developments are fused into a single pattern.

The third stage in the Private Gentleman's spiritual deterioration is no more than an extension of the preceding one, but it is worth mentioning separately because it involves an interesting shift in metaphor. In their initial rebellion, both Crusoe and the Private Gentleman appear as Prodigal Sons; in their subsequent flight, both are shown as afflicted mariners;

[9] The primary meaning of "castaway," as late as the era of Johnson's dictionary, is "A person lost or abandoned by Providence"; see I Cor. 9:27.

finally, at their highest pitch of callous defiance, both are likened to Balaam. It will be recalled that the prophet sets out on an expedition that God has expressly forbidden. Angered at this disobedience, God sends an angel to block Balaam's way. Three times the ass on which Balaam is riding sees the angel, and tries to turn aside or stop, but Balaam himself is as blind to this warning as he had been deaf to God's original command. At last Balaam's eyes are opened, and he sees the angel of the Lord standing in his way, sword in hand. The angel explains, "I went out to withstand thee, because thy way was perverse before me," and declares that nothing but the ass's turning has saved Balaam from being slain. At all of this Balaam is much abashed, and henceforth attends God's will (Numbers 22:12–35). Crusoe has virtually the same experience; an encounter with a threatening angel marks a turning point in his own spiritual career. There are variations in detail, but, as will be shown later, these do not lessen the basic similarity.

As it happens, the Private Gentleman is no more confronted by an angel than he is shipwrecked. Yet he uses the Balaam story in the same way, as an image of his spiritual strait. Speaking of his insensitivity to the plainest Providential warnings, he says, "Like the Prophet, more brutish than the Ass he rode on, I spurr'd on, tho' a flaming Sword of Vengeance was brandish'd before my Face." [10] Thus it is the earlier

[10] *Account*, p. 58. Another author alludes to the same episode in describing his own progress in sin: "Thus far have I gone, and in all probability much farther had I proceeded, if my merciful God, by a strong and irresistible providence, had not stood in the way and resisted me; for nothing less would conquer my stubborn and masterless Nature" (*An Alarme*

portion of the story, not its conclusion, that he alludes
to: he resembles Balaam only in obtuseness, and has yet
to come to his senses. The simile adds no new dimension to his picture of youthful impiety, but it does
suggest a final, culminating degree of waywardness.

After such prolonged and aggravated truancy, the
eventual return to self-awareness is bound to be painful, and so it proves in the *Account*. As the Private
Gentleman observes, " 'tis *Satan's* great Artifice to let
us see no Sin, or all Sin; to ruin by Presumption, or
Despair: And strangely surprizing and amazing is it, to
pass from a State of Insensibility, to feel the Load of
insupportable Guilt." [11] These sensations were frequently reported in the traditional spiritual autobiographies, where they were referred to as "Troubles of
Mind" or a "wounded Spirit." With some notable
exceptions, however, such experiences were not ordinarily treated at much length, perhaps for the simple
reason that they usually occur just before conversion.
An autobiographer will mention them as the labor
pains that inevitably precede the new birth, and hasten
on to discuss the climactic conversion itself.[12] Once

*for Sinners: Containing The Confession, Prayers, Letters, and
last Words of Robert Foulkes, Late Minister of Stanton-Lacy
in the County of Salop; who was Tryed, Convicted, and
Sentenced, at the Sessions in the Old Bayly, London, January
16th 1678/9, and Executed the 31st following* [1679], p. 13).

[11] *Account*, p. 23. This principle is restated at several points
in the book: see pp. 55, 223–24.

[12] Autobiographers were not alone in discussing conversion
in terms of new birth; indeed, they could employ the analogy
dramatically, without pausing to explain its spiritual significance, precisely because John 3:3–7 and the other pertinent
texts were explored so often in sermons and treatises. Nevertheless Margaret Bottrall finds remarkable the dream of re-

capable of "serious consideration," once arrived at "conviction of sin," his delivery was imminent; God seldom left him wallowing long in this state of anguish, but would come to his relief like the father of the returning prodigal. In the *Account*, on the other hand, "Trouble of Mind" becomes the main subject. Its position in the conventional structure is not altered, since it retains a place between the stages of sin and regeneration.[13] Yet there is a major shift in emphasis: what had often been a brief transitional phase here occupies the greater part of a three-hundred-page book. The description of prolonged distress dominates the narrative, not only by its sheer volume, but by its minute probing of each variation in the form or intensity of affliction. Up to this point the Private Gentleman is disturbingly reticent about the actual details of his life. Instead of a direct, circumstantial account of his doings and sufferings, he offers a series of metaphors and allusions; and much as these might enrich and elucidate a factual narrative, they cannot simply replace it, as they are made to do in the early part of the *Account*. But in this central section of the book the Private Gentleman temporarily achieves that balance between narration and interpretation which was pro-

generation in *Grace Abounding*, "expressed in terms which so closely correspond to the experience of physical birth"; the credit is given to Bunyan's "instinct for imagery deeply rooted in common physical experience," when in fact he deserves praise rather for employing quite conventional imagery in a fresh, vigorous way (*Every Man a Phoenix* [1958], pp. 103–04).

[13] The term "Trouble of Mind" was also applied at times to the doubts and fears that may follow conversion. See Timothy Rogers, *A Discourse Concerning Trouble of Mind, and The Disease of Melancholly* (1691). Such trouble of mind occupies the bulk of *Grace Abounding*.

posed earlier as the fundamental criterion of successful spiritual autobiography.[14]

For reasons suggested above, an autobiographer will seldom give equal weight to the periods that precede and follow conversion: one who has attained conversion after long weltering in a natural state will say little about later backslidings, while one who has been converted early in life will fill his narrative with later temptations and slackenings. In the *Account*, the phase of despair is so enlarged that both the prior state of sin and the subsequent state of regeneration get relatively meager attention. As a result, the inverse proportion that generally obtains between the portraits of sin and regeneration is not so much upset as superseded, in this instance, by the emergence of a third element that stunts both the others. But if the account of eventual regeneration is rather perfunctory in comparison with the treatment of "Trouble of Mind," it is nevertheless interesting as an example of the continuity of themes between genuine spiritual autobiography and the fiction to come. Various motifs which had long been associated with regeneration, and which were to figure in Defoe's works of the following decade, appear here as traits of the Private Gentleman's ultimate recovery.

Just as the clearest symptoms of his spiritual unsoundness had been a rebellion against Providential disposition, followed by a disregard of Providential attempts to humble and reform him, so the main

[14] The story of long and varied bouts with despair also makes a noteworthy contribution to the literature of "The English Malady"; see Cecil A. Moore's essay on the subject in *Backgrounds of English Literature, 1700–1760* (Minneapolis, 1953), pp. 179–235.

outward token of his renewed spiritual health is an acknowledgment of Providence, involving acquiescence in what it determines and keen attention to what it directs. Before he had been tossed, as he puts it, with "many Storms of Temptations, that often threatned to overset me, and must, had not a kind Hand of Providence continually trim'd the Vessel: Few were my Halcyon Days, and those commonly prov'd the Harbingers of blustring Seasons; but alas, all this while, I little thought from what Quarter the Wind blew" (p. 77). His real misfortune had not been the "Storms of Temptations" or the other kinds of "blustring Seasons," but the failure to see "from what Quarter the Wind blew": the failure, in other words, to perceive that it was the hand of Providence punishing yet preserving him, and rousing him in order to reclaim him. Even after his conversion, the Private Gentleman is not altogether rid of "blustring Seasons." His regeneration cannot prevent them, but it does enable him to cope with them.

The difference, then, is not that he now enjoys uninterrupted tranquillity, but that he can trace and heed God's doing in all that happens to him.[15] In the blindness of his unregenerate state, he had tended to ascribe events to mere fate, chance, or the operation of natural causes. Now he is able and alert to detect a divine influence in outwardly random occurrences, and a first cause behind the mechanical sequence of second causes. As a consequence, he no longer looks

[15] "I could now see and observe God in his Providence; in Sermons, suiting his Word to my Wants; in my ordinary Conversation; in Dangers, Deliverances; in Afflictions, Mercies; in the works of Nature and Grace; in publick and private Converses. To all which, and much more, I found myself stark blind before" (*Account*, p. 210).

vainly to the world for satisfaction ("My affections, once spread like Dung on the Face of the Earth, I felt now centering in their proper Object" [p. 214]), or to his own efforts and abilities for its attainment: "Act in all kinds with vigor," he exhorts, "but still in humble Dependance; lay failings at your own Door, but ever ascribe Successes to God: If you trust or applaud Self, a fall will ensue, the Glory of his Grace he will have, or of his Justice" (p. 196).

Here the Private Gentleman raises an issue which later fictional works like *Robinson Crusoe* were to explore more fully. If the unregenerate man's self-reliance was vain, the regenerate man's dependence on God could also be carried to excess. If the former erred in trusting to his own efforts and abilities, thus denying God's power to sanction or thwart whatever he attempted, the latter might be equally rash in relaxing or abandoning his exertions, and fondly assuming that God's care made his own labor unnecessary. Both extremes are obviously imprudent, yet both are impious as well; it is less obvious that over-dependence should be so, but the explanation is actually quite simple. "To use means," as one writer puts it, "without respect to God, is proudly to contemn him; to depend upon God without the use of means, is irreligiously to tempt him; in both we abuse his Providence." [16] The

---

[16] Stephen Charnock, "A Treatise of Divine Providence," in *Works*, 3rd edition (1699), p. 531. A fuller explanation of this principle is to be found in a sermon by Daniel Waterland entitled "Wicked Men, the providential Instruments of Good," in his *Works*, 6 vols. (Oxford, 1856), V, 489–90. The Private Gentleman himself states the matter as follows: "Some despise Means, others dote on them, both are extreams very faulty and dangerous, and tho' so distant, yet they often beget one the other thro' Humane frailty: The one tempts God, the other neglects him: The one nullifies the Creature, the

implications of this view are important for the interpretation of *Robinson Crusoe*, and will be seen in the later discussion of that book. As for the *Account*, it is enough to remark that the Private Gentleman neither advocates nor embodies the notion that a man's welfare consists in his industry: on the contrary, he censures such an attitude for doting on means, neglecting God, idolizing the creature, and pinning faith entirely upon second causes. Far from asserting the dignity of labor, he argues merely for its necessity; far from writing a panegyric of work, he pleads merely for "humble Dependance" in the worker.

At any rate, the foremost token of his regeneration is the discovery that he is an object of Providential concern and care. This realization does not betray him into sloth, however; it rather provokes him to new diligence and activity, for he sees that he must strike a middle course between total reliance on either Providence or himself. Although he trusts to Providence for support, and looks to it for direction, he does not make the mistake of supposing that his own efforts are superseded. Although reduced to greater humility and dependence, he acquires new strength and confidence.

Having reached this state himself, he is a fit person to help those who are as he had been. By recounting his own spiritual career, he may "awaken the Presumptuous, convince the Sceptick, and encourage the Despondent," as the title of his book undertakes to do.

---

other Idolizeth it: The one will have God at his beck to work Miracles, and change the course of Nature to relieve him; the other will have nothing to do with him, but pins his Faith entirely upon second Causes; is not the Medium clear and plain, as evident as the Light?" (p. 125; see also Appendix).

The preceding chapter has shown that a willingness to benefit others by an account of one's own experience was regarded as a natural consequence of conversion. In this light, the *Account* itself constitutes a further token of the Private Gentleman's regeneration. His renewed spiritual health permits and prompts him to treat those who are still ailing; the story of his own malady and its cure constitutes an attempt to help others diagnose and remedy their ills. Here both narrative and reflections play their parts. The narrative charts out initial symptoms, gradual complications, crisis, and recovery in the Private Gentleman's case, thus enabling readers to recognize their own conditions and proceed accordingly; the reflections prescribe more explicitly what is to be done or avoided.

The second token of the Private Gentleman's regeneration, then, is this impulse to instruct and exhort others. The essentially didactic character of the traditional spiritual autobiography was discussed earlier; however much the *Account* may modify or depart from certain other conventions of the genre, it fully retains this one. The very preface establishes the primacy of edification: "After all, if the Historick part be frown'd upon in point of Truth, as fact; or reality, as represented in the following Discourse, (a thing not at all unusual in Matters of this Nature) 'tis hop'd some serious Truths here deliver'd, may be of some use to well disposed Persons." [17]

But unlike some later fictional works, which would pose as spiritual autobiographies and make similar pro-

---

[17] "The Publisher to the Reader," p. [iv]; cf. also Preface, p. vii: "*The Stile is not polite, nor is the Method calculated to please the Sons of Art: my Business is not to amuse, but edifie; which engages me to write in as familiar Terms as possible.*"

testations, the *Account* actually does subordinate the "Historick part" to "serious Truths"; the narrative exists to give the reflections cogency through example.[18] In fact, a readiness at every turn to postpone action for the sake of more or less serious reflections is to be found in rather extreme form in the *Account*. But in this feature it differs little from its antecedents, the genuine spiritual autobiographies: in works like Fraser's *Memoirs*, homiletic "improvement" had constantly threatened to grow out of proportion to its narrative matrix.

The final mark of the Private Gentleman's regeneration is closely connected with the preceding one. Spiritual autobiographies traditionally combined a didactic with an autodidactic function; much the same combination is to be found in the *Account*. If one mark of the regenerate man was a keenness to recount his past vicissitudes for the benefit of others, it was equally characteristic that he should examine and interpret further experiences, just as they occurred, for his own benefit. Even if his spiritual life were to become uninterruptedly tranquil, gratitude would oblige him to acknowledge the blessing, so that he

[18] Although the Private Gentleman's reflections vary in length from aphorisms of a few lines to essays of several pages, they frequently consist of such Crusoesque paragraphs as this (pp. 221-22): "And is God indeed thus Merciful, thus ready to forgive the greatest Sinners, and able to relieve in the most deplorable Exigency, even after Sins against the brightest Means? against Principles of Education, Light and Conviction, Mercies most endearing, Warnings, Providences, Judgments, thro' a continued series of many Years, at the expence of the greatest Goodness and Patience slighted and abus'd? Who then has any reason, or dare Despair, after such a Precedent, if he be but willing to return to God and his Duty?"

might continue to deserve it. If on the other hand he was subjected to new trials and temptations, or even to weakenings in his own assurance of grace, prudence would compel him to continue or resume his self-scrutiny, in order to recover the peace enjoyed at conversion. In other words, whether he was faring well or badly, the regenerate man would be bound continually to review the state of his soul. Diary-keeping had long been an esteemed way of carrying out these required self-assessments, and by undertaking one of his own, the Private Gentleman gives further evidence of the spiritual soundness he has attained.[19]

The omissions in this portrait of regeneration, like those in Fraser's account of conversion, are as significant as its inclusions. Though the Private Gentleman is presumably still in the metropolis, he has nothing to say about the effect of his new state on his dealings with others; except for counselling and catechizing his readers, he seems isolated from all human contacts. As a result, there are certain manifestations of spiritual rebirth about which he is noticeably silent: the discharge of relative duties and the exercise of charity are topics omitted from the account of his new life. Apart from the effort to enlighten others, embodied in the *Account* itself, his new condition has no

[19] "Diaries are grown much out of Fashion, but their natural usefulness, and the Example of some holy Souls, persuaded me now to attempt something of that nature. For want of this, I run over Head and Ears in Accounts with Heaven, and had nothing to fly to in my Distress, but was in perfect Confusion. Had I set about this sooner, I had not been so great a Stranger to Self-Examination, a faithful Monitor, the best preventive Exercise to keep the Soul from running deep into the Debt of Divine Justice; nor consequently had I prov'd such a Bankrupt as I found my self, even to amazement" (p. 244).

public, external dimension: it consists wholly in a reshaping of his private, internal bearing towards God.[20]

Again the analogy with Crusoe is interesting. The Private Gentleman seems as alone in London as Crusoe on his island; while Crusoe's solitude is the more literal, the Private Gentleman's is no less real. The process of regeneration brings each of them into closer, more harmonious relation with God, but leaves both of them as remote as ever from the rest of mankind. Both are "alone," then, so far as human contact is concerned, yet neither feels as isolated or forsaken as he had before conversion. Crusoe happens upon the Biblical assurance, "I will never, never leave thee, nor forsake thee," and the sense of this attachment consoles him for the lack of all others. The same sense of God's presence affects the Private Gentleman, so that without withdrawing bodily from society he becomes something of a recluse in spirit. Crusoe neither goes to the island for religious motives, nor does he ever really relish his solitude, much as he finds to compensate for his loneliness: thus he is never more truly a hermit than the Private Gentleman, who remains in the world but not of it. More will be said of solitude in the discussion of *Robinson Crusoe;* here it is enough to observe that the treatment of this theme in Defoe's *Serious Reflections* is just as relevant to the Private Gentleman as to Crusoe.

[20] It is characteristic that the Private Gentleman should twice observe, "Happy is the Man that practically understands these Three blessed Duties; of Watchfulness, Prayer, and Dependance" (p. 15; cf. p. 216). These are duties that bind man to God, or at most to God's doings in the world; they do not bind him to fellow man, as would the obligation of charity.

If the Private Gentleman's solitude within society is curiously akin to Crusoe's outside it, there is a further resemblance in the way the solitude of each is broken: but as with other experiences common to both of them, this happens more literally in Crusoe's case than in the Private Gentleman's. Just as each had acted the prodigal, although only Crusoe had sallied from home, wandered abroad, and suffered hardship, so too each ends his solitude, although only Crusoe encounters a Friday. The Private Gentleman's release from solitude is not an event in his narrative; it is the very act of delivering his narrative. It is not a shift from soliloquy to dialogue, as with Crusoe, but from silence to monologue. The Presumptuous, the Sceptick, and the Despondent, to whom the *Account* is addressed at the outset, tend to disappear from view in the course of the book, rather like the Ancient Mariner's wedding guest; yet the Private Gentleman continues to instruct and exhort whoever stays with him. In effect, then, the reader is to the Private Gentleman what Friday is to Crusoe. Both the Private Gentleman and Crusoe obey the regenerate man's normal impulse to edify the natural man: the difference is that the Private Gentleman does so largely in the manner of the traditional spiritual autobiographer, appealing directly to his readers, while Crusoe does so within the narrative, through the medium of Friday. The difference, in other words, is one of technical sophistication. Technical sophistication is no doubt the last quality one would ordinarily attribute to Crusoe's instruction of Friday: here if anywhere one seems to be faced with Defoe's well-known artlessness. Taken by itself, the scene certainly is one of charming naïveté; yet measured against an appropriate background—the autobiographical tradition of the regenerate teaching the unregenerate—it comes to appear very skillfully contrived.[21] In the *Account*, as indeed in Defoe's own *Serious Reflections*, instruction gets detached from narration: in *Robinson Crusoe* they are one, and Defoe's ingenuity consists precisely in this ability to unite them.

The following chapter will show in detail how Defoe unites narration and instruction; what has mattered here is the transitional character of the *Account* itself. Structurally, it differs little from earlier autobiography, since it adheres to the traditional sequence of spiritual developments, and alters only their relative weight or prominence. The same basic structure is to be found in *Robinson Crusoe*: the hero's vicissitudes, highly individual and complex as they appear to be, actually follow a conventional and regular pattern of spiritual evolution. But if the *Account* serves to illustrate the formal continuity between spiritual autobiography and such works as *Robinson Crusoe*, it also points up some important contrasts. The Private Gentleman, like most of the autobiographers before him, dwells at length on the spiritual significance of his every action, sometimes to the virtual exclusion of actual narrative. Defoe, on the other hand, by leading his hero through a series of conventionally meaningful actions, fuses a great deal of interpretation and comment into the narrative itself.

The differences, of course, are not as clear-cut as this would suggest. It has been shown that the *Account* does at times speak metaphorically of experiences like

[21] For a different approach to this scene, not incompatible with the present one, see J. Paul Hunter, "Friday as a Convert: Defoe and the Accounts of Indian Missionaries," *RES*, XIV (1963), pp. 243–48.

Crusoe's, and the following chapter will point out various passages in which Defoe becomes quite as explicit about what things mean as the author of the *Account*. In other words, *Robinson Crusoe* is by no means the first book in which rebelling against paternal authority, rambling abroad, becoming enslaved, getting shipwrecked, etc., take on spiritual significance. On the contrary, they had long possessed such overtones. Yet it remained for Defoe to integrate their narrative and spiritual elements as completely, or on such a scale, as he does in *Robinson Crusoe*.

CHAPTER III

Robinson Crusoe

I. CRUSOE'S "ORIGINAL SIN"

Crusoe's running away to sea has long intrigued readers. Within months of the book's original appearance, Defoe's treatment of the incident was challenged: Charles Gildon was the first to object that Defoe presents as sinful a deed which seems at worst a mild offense, if not altogether justifiable, and that he ascribes to it consequences which seem out of all proportion to its gravity, even if one were to grant its culpability.[1] Modern commentators react less indignantly than Gildon, but they continue to feel that Defoe's handling of the matter requires explanation. Both Crusoe's motivation in leaving home, and Defoe's reason for labelling the act a sin, have been variously interpreted in recent years.

According to Maximillian Novak, "the rationale for this action may be found in Crusoe's personal characteristics: his lack of economic prudence, his inability to follow a steady profession, his indifference to a calm bourgeois life, and his love of travel."[2] In stressing these "personal characteristics," however, Mr. Novak,

[1] *The Life and Strange Surprizing Adventures of Mr. D. . . . . De F . . . of London, Hosier . . .* (1719); edited by Paul Dottin as *Robinson Crusoe Examin'd and Criticis'd . . .* (London and Paris, 1923), pp. 82–87.

[2] *Economics and the Fiction of Daniel Defoe* (Berkeley and Los Angeles, 1962), p. 32.

it seems to me, reads into the account a rather more individualized portrait than Defoe actually gives us at this stage of the book. Four years before the appearance of *Robinson Crusoe*, Defoe had assessed the temperament of youth as follows: *"Folly that is bound up in the Heart of a Child*, says Solomon, *is driven by the Rod of Correction. . . . What this folly is,* needs no Description here, other than an allow'd Custom in doing Evil, a natural Propensity we all have to Evil; with this we are all born into the world, the Soul is originally bent to Folly." [3] In the last book he wrote, Defoe was to observe that "men are in their youth hurry'd down the stream of their worst affeccions by the meer insensible impetuosity of nature." [4] The mo-

---

[3] *Family Instructor*, I, 68. Compare *Mere Nature Delineated; Or, A Body without a Soul* (1726), in which Defoe asks, "why does Meer Nature lead to foolish Things by the Course of its own Instinct? Why hurry the Soul down the Stream of his Affections, and, with inexpressible Gust, to what is gross, sordid, and brutish; whereas Wisdom and virtuous Principles are all up Hill, against the Stream, and are rather acquir'd than natural? Let those who deny original Depravity, answer this for me, if they think they can; for my Part, I acknowledge it to be out of my Reach, upon any other foot" (p. 44). In *Religious Courtship* Defoe similarly declares that "nature prompts us to evil thoughts and evil desires, and to them only; the imagination of the thoughts of our hearts are evil, and only evil; if there are any good motions, or heavenly desires in the heart, they are from God" (p. 55).

[4] *The Compleat English Gentleman*, edited by K. D. Bülbring (1890), p. 111. Cf. also *Serious Reflections*, pp. 104, 267; *Review*, Nov. 4, 1704, edited in facsimile by Arthur W. Secord, 22 vols. (N.Y., 1938), I, 294; *Little Review*, June 22, 1705, pp. 21-22; *A New Discovery of an Old Intreague: A Satyr levell'd at Treachery and Ambition*, in *A Second Volume of the Writings of the Author of the True-Born Englishman* (1705), p. 19. H. H. Andersen discusses the matter in "The Paradox of Trade and Morality in Defoe," *MP*, xxxix (1941), pp. 29, 43.

tives he imputes to Robinson Crusoe do not, I think, amount to more than this. That man is naturally subject to rebellious impulse is a principle he frequently asserts, and it would appear to provide a sufficient "rationale" for Crusoe's behavior on this occasion. Indeed, the episode seems to rest on an orthodox Calvinistic conception of man's innate waywardness and obstinacy. Obadiah Grew, an ejected Presbyterian minister like those under whom Defoe was educated, expresses the traditional belief in his assertion that "every man by nature hath a lusting desire to leave God, and live at his own hand; he would stand on his own legs and bottom, and be at his own dispose: Thus it is with every man by Nature . . . Man would be at liberty from God and his Will, to follow and fulfill his own; *Man is born like a wild Asses Colt;* vain man is so, saith *Zophar*. He hath a *principium laesum*, a devillish principle in his nature; an impulse to range about the earth, as Satan said of himself." [5] Crusoe's father admonishes him "not to play the young man," and a generalized portrait of the young man as "wild Asses Colt" is, in effect, what we are given at the outset, rather than individual traits. [6]

[5] *Meditations Upon our Saviour's Parable of the Prodigal Son* (1678), pp. 44, 46; cf. John Goodman, *The Penitent Pardoned*, p. 85; Ezekiel Hopkins, *Works*, p. 525.

[6] What Mr. Novak describes in positive terms as "a love of travel" should perhaps be regarded merely as Crusoe's initial manifestation of the impulse Grew deplores. Similarly, his "inability to follow a steady profession" and his "indifference to a calm bourgeois life" may be viewed as incidental effects of this inborn and universal tendency, rather than "personal characteristics." One has similar reservations about his suggested "lack of economic prudence": it may be one corollary of his *principium laesum*, but it is hard to see in what sense it is a trait of personality that contributes to his running away.

On this reading, then, Crusoe is motivated by the wildness that Defoe found characteristic of unregenerate man in general, and of youth in particular, rather than the "personal characteristics" suggested by Mr. Novak.

Mr. Novak further maintains that Crusoe's sin consists in "his refusal to follow the 'calling' chosen for him by his father"; Cotton Mather and Richard Norwood are cited in support of the view that Crusoe's action violates this specific "religious-economic doctrine." [7] By drawing attention to a religious implication of the deed, Mr. Novak's study provides a useful caveat against exclusively economic interpretations.[8] But his own argument is weakened, it seems to me, by narrowing Crusoe's sin to a violation of this particular doctrine. Implicit in Defoe's treatment of the episode is a conventional identification of family, social and divine order, all of which are flouted by Crusoe's deed. Since human affairs are governed by Providence, any attempt to disrupt or elude their established pattern implies a denial of God's power and, by extension,

[7] *Economics* . . . , pp. 32, 40 and *passim*. On the concept of the calling, see Max Weber, *The Protestant Ethic and The Spirit of Capitalism* (N.Y., 1958), pp. 79f., 161f.; and R. H. Tawney, *Religion and The Rise of Capitalism* (N.Y., 1963), pp. 199-202.

[8] Ian Watt, for instance, maintains that Crusoe runs away "for the classic reason of *homo economicus*—that it is necessary to better his economic condition." It is "economic individualism," according to Watt, that "prevents Crusoe from paying much heed to the ties of family." As he points out, Crusoe reflects that "there seemed to be something fatal in that propension of nature" which overruled these family ties; nevertheless Watt regards the episode as the first instance of that economic motivation which he finds actuating Crusoe throughout the book. See *The Rise of the Novel* (Berkeley and Los Angeles, 1957), pp. 65, 66 and *passim*.

challenges his very existence.[9] The virtual equation between paternal and divine authority is too commonplace to require discussion; it rests, of course, on the fifth commandment and on Deuteronomy 27:16, a text which Defoe uses to good effect elsewhere.[10]

It is worth glancing briefly, however, at the extraordinary interest Providence takes in the "middle station in life." Crusoe's father extolls the upper station of low life as the best state in the world and the most suited to human happiness, pointing out that "the wise man gave his testimony to this as the just standard of true felicity, when he prayed to have neither poverty nor riches." He alludes to Agur's prayer (Proverbs 30:8-9): "give me neither poverty nor riches; feed me with food convenient for me: Lest I be full, and deny thee, and say Who is the Lord? or lest I be poor, and steal, and take the name of my God in vain." This theme was a favorite with contemporary moralists,[11]

[9] This line of argument is a commonplace in treatises on Providence: see T[homas] C[rane], *Isagoge ad Dei Providentiam: or, a Prospect of Divine Providence* (1672), pp. 507–09; Stephen Charnock, "A Treatise of Divine Providence," in *Works*, 3rd edition (1699), p. 533. Defoe makes a similar point in *Serious Reflections*, pp. 191–92.

[10] See Part II of *The Family Instructor*, p. 243, where the despairing brother is made to say, "I remember that terrible Scripture with many a Reproach upon myself, *Cursed be he that setteth light by his Father and Mother.*"

[11] See *A Supplement to the Athenian Oracle* (1706), p. 290; Lady Frances (Freke) Norton, *The Applause of Virtue* (1705), pp. 255–56; *Husbandry Spiritualized*, in the *Whole Works of the Reverend Mr. John Flavel*, 2 vols. (Glasgow, 1754), II, 169; *The Works of the Pious and Profoundly Learned Joseph Mede* (1664), pp. 167–81; *The Works of Francis Osborne, Esq.*, 8th edition (1682), pp. 514, 518, and *passim*. In *The Early Masters of English Fiction* (Lawrence, 1956), Mr. McKillop notes a further expression of this idea in a sermon by Benjamin Hoadly (p. 2).

and Defoe reiterates it at various points in his writings.[12] It is true that Crusoe would have been under an equal obligation to accept his lot had his father been poor or rich, a laborer or a peer. His action is made to appear all the more rash and willful, however, by the very fact that he has been placed, as his father points out, "in the middle of the two extremes, between the mean and the great." He, cannot plead the ignorance or want that extenuate the misdeeds of the poor, or the forgetfulness amid excess that plagues the rich; he is neither driven by necessity nor lulled by surfeit. Since wealth and poverty are equally beset by spiritual hazards, Providence has shown a special fondness for the English middle class by sparing it the temptations into which both extremes are led. In repudiating such a blessing, Crusoe—like the Prodigal Son before him—displays no mere "lack of economic prudence," but a radical perversity and impiety.

By a single act, Crusoe thus defies the joint authority of family, society, and Providence. If we bear in mind these multiple sanctions against rebellion, the question of the intrinsic enormity of running off to sea loses its relevance. In itself, the act may be somewhat more complex than, say, eating an apple, yet each deed is significant primarily as an outward token of a spiritual state. In a sense, Crusoe's original sin does cause his later misfortunes; from another point of view, it is merely the first overt expression of a more fundamental source of trouble: the natural waywardness of every unregenerate man. It "causes" what follows in

[12] Compare *Moll Flanders*, I, 200; *Review*, III, 110a; *Compleat English Gentleman*, pp. 102–03; *Serious Reflections*, p. 33f.; and especially *The Compleat English Tradesman*, 2nd edition, 2 vols. (1727), II, 193–94.

that each step towards damnation necessarily leads to the next, unless conversion intervenes: thus Crusoe's option of altering his headstrong course is renewed on several subsequent occasions, but he repeats and aggravates his initial error. The running off to sea is not, in other words, the direct cause of all later vicissitudes, but it does initiate a pattern of wrongdoing which has far-reaching consequences. To use another analogy, Jonah's running away to sea does in a sense cause his later misfortunes; that is, it largely determines the outward form of the subsequent narrative. Like Crusoe's embarkation for London, Jonah's embarkation for Tarshish proves disastrous. Yet it is Jonah's fundamental rebelliousness, not the specific form which his insubordination takes, that provokes the divine wrath.

Of both Crusoe's and Jonah's first disobedience it can be said that the outward deed expresses admirably the inward state of the hero. Both acts, along with the prodigal's departure into a far country, manage to present a spiritual condition in concrete terms. In each case the initial casting off of restraint not only sets in motion a narrative interesting in its own right but also provides a kind of "objective correlative" for the hero's turbulent, unruly spirit. Other objectifications of Crusoe's spiritual state were available; the literature of sin is rich in metaphor, and the account of Crusoe's doings prior to conversion employs a number of them, some only allusively and in passing, others more extensively as integral parts of the narrative. When certain divines came to describe the nature of sin, they gave what were in effect catalogues of such metaphors. Obadiah Sedgwick, for example, asserts that "Every sinfull man is a wandring Meteor, a very Planet on earth; he is gone from the fold, as a silly sheep; he is gone from his Fathers house, as a silly Child; he is gone out of the right path, like a silly Traveller in the Wilderness. Sin puts us into a Maze, into a Labyrinth; we go from one sin to another sin, out of one by-path into another by-path; and the further we go in sinfull paths, the more still we go out of the way." [13]

As preceding chapters have shown, it was quite common for spiritual autobiographers to weave such motifs into their recollections, in order to illustrate the nature and extent of their sinfulness prior to conversion. In *Robinson Crusoe* Defoe develops such motifs to the point that they become the very fabric of his narrative. Although they take on a vitality of their own in the process, they nevertheless retain their original and basic metaphorical function.

2. CRUSOE ERRANT

I have suggested that the economic impulses postulated by Mr. Watt and the "personal characteristics" cited by Mr. Novak may have less to do with Crusoe's running away than the sheer rebelliousness and obstinacy which Defoe found in youth generally, and which he ascribes to Crusoe in particular. In my opinion, Crusoe's initial motivation is no more concealed or complex than Robert Drury's, as Defoe describes it in the opening pages of *Madagascar:*

"NOTWITHSTANDING all the Education my Father bestow'd on me, I cou'd not be brought to think of any Art, Science, Trade, Business, or Profession of any kind whatsoever, but *Going to Sea:* And as soon as I was capable of answering any Questions propounded to me, concerning what Business or Profession my

[13] *Parable of the Prodigal*, p. 236.

Genius led me to, I discover'd no Inclination to any thing but *the Sea*. And I well remember, that from Eleven Years of Age, my Mind had taken such an unhappy Bent this Way, that it grew with my Stature, and at length became an obstinate Resolution; and not all the tender Insinuations of my dear and indulgent Mother, tho' she once intreated me on her Knees, nor the Perswasions of my tender Father, and other Friends, could make any Impression on me.

"WHEN they found their Endeavours were in vain, they then try'd another Method, and by a seeming Compliance with my Desire, did propose, and would have procur'd a short Voyage for me; hoping that the Dangers I should be liable to, and the Hardships I should see others suffer, would terrify me from persisting in that Course of Life. But,

"SUCH was my unhappy Obstinacy, that nothing would serve me, but what was for my Ruin; and Providence herein justly punish'd my Disobedience, by granting me the foolish Choice I had wickedly made, in direct Opposition to my Duty, and the earnest Entreaties of my Friends. Thus did this Perverseness of mine bring along with it its own Pains and Punishment." [14]

Here an "Inclination" becomes an "unhappy Bent," develops into an "obstinate Resolution," and issues in "Disobedience" and "Perverseness." Bearing in mind the assumptions about human nature discussed in the preceding section, we need no more elaborate explanation of why either Drury or Crusoe goes to sea.

I have also maintained that the sinfulness of the deed consists in its violation of paternal, social, and divine

[14] *Madagascar: Or, Robert Drury's Journal, During Fifteen Years Captivity on that Island* (1729), pp. 2–3.

order; that its wickedness is emphasized by the resemblance to similar acts of rebellion committed by Jonah and the Prodigal Son; and that the account of Crusoe's subsequent vicissitudes employs other conventional metaphors for spiritual states, with important effects on the book's literary and religious qualities alike. Here I shall trace Crusoe's career up to the point of conversion.

Discussions of *Robinson Crusoe* commonly focus on the island existence, and the "original sin" has also attracted attention, but the intervening wanderings tend to be passed over. Considered simply as narrative, however, this phase of the book deserves some scrutiny, for from one point of view it is curiously brief, from another it is oddly extended. Why does Defoe have so little to say about Sallee and Brazil, and yet detain Crusoe so long from reaching the island? For all his interest in circumstantial realism, Defoe takes few pains to "place" Crusoe in Sallee, about which there was a considerable literature, or in Brazil, which was also adequately described. Crusoe's stay in Sallee occupies less than five pages, which mainly concern his devices to escape; little is said about the city or his life there, and even less space is devoted to his four years in Brazil. In such travel-narratives as *Captain Singleton* and the *Farther Adventures of Robinson Crusoe*, Defoe's zest for factual detail seldom flags; in this book, it is largely reserved for the island. Despite the availability of ample material on Barbary slavery and Brazilian settlement, he neglects these opportunities to display his powers of narrative realism.

It could be argued that he is primarily concerned to get Crusoe to the island, but that, to bring him into the neighborhood with some show of plausibility, he must contrive this sequence of preliminary stages. Robert Drury can be shipwrecked on Madagascar within thirteen pages of the beginning of a book because Madagascar is in fact on the route to India; if Crusoe is to be isolated from the normal paths of commerce the preparations have to be rather more elaborate.

But there are other reasons, I think, why it is nearly fifty pages before Crusoe clambers ashore on his island. For one thing, his habitat becomes more and more remote from his native Yorkshire, until at last it is a place found on no map. Earlier discussion of the *Account* showed how the author, who in fact remains in London throughout the book, expresses his estrangement from God through metaphors of physical distance: he speaks of himself as wandering, straying, fleeing, hiding, and rambling in order to convey his inward, spiritual remoteness from "the true center of his being." What we have in Crusoe's case, I think, is a full enactment of this process in the outward narrative. Instead of merely likening himself to one in this predicament, Crusoe actually undergoes such wanderings, yet they seem to retain their traditional overtones of alienation. The background of this identification between literal and spiritual wandering has already been presented and need not be recapitulated; instead we may turn to another possible reason for Crusoe's delay in reaching the island.

However impious and imprudent it may be, his decision to venture abroad is entirely voluntary; he is neither tricked like Colonel Jack nor forced by law like Moll Flanders into embarking on his voyage. Nevertheless he has remarkably little control over the direction of his travels. Not only is his judgment tainted, even at the time of his initial misstep, but choice of any kind, rational or otherwise, has less and less power over his affairs. This process of subjection, first of reason to rebellious inclination, next of action in general to external circumstances, traditionally marks the worsening predicament of unregenerate man.

That Crusoe actually undergoes such a process can perhaps be best illustrated by the Barbary slavery episode. In attempting to repeat the success of his first trading voyage to Guinea, he is captured by pirates and carried to Sallee. As already indicated, Defoe shows little interest in developing the narrative possibilities of Crusoe's captivity, although model accounts were available to him, and he had long been interested in African affairs. There was one feature of the slavery accounts, however, which was more to Defoe's purpose than their descriptive details. They all tended to be written from the same motives: namely, to return thanks for the author's ultimate escape or redemption, and to celebrate the workings of a beneficent Providence even amid the remote, benighted Moors.[15] Even when the bulk of a narrative consisted of exotic topography, fabulous natural history, and prodigious action, as in *The Adventures of Mr. T. S. an English Merchant* (1670), it was deemed appropriate to begin as follows: "There is nothing appears more wonderful than Gods Providence in the Governance of the World, and in the disposition of Mankind; it carries us through various Estates; it brings us in Dangers and Miseries, and in a due time leads us out again by means not discoverable to our shallow foresight; it causeth us

[15] These narratives are discussed in my forthcoming article in *HLQ*, "Escape from Barbary: A Seventeenth-Century Genre."

to meet with such different Accidents, which some may attribute to Chance; but if we take the pains to examine and question them, we shall find them to be appointed by a Divine Wisdom for the Publick and our own Advantage. . . . Modern and Ancient Histories are full of such strange Examples of the Proceedings of Providence, which tend many times only to fashion and frame us to a certain temper that may make us more useful in our Generations" (pp. 1–3).

Now this is just the kind of reflection that Crusoe comes to make after his conversion, but at the time of his captivity and escape he is blind to the agency of Providence in his affairs. He does feel at first that "now the hand of heaven had overtaken me, and I was undone without redemption," but beyond this he makes no spiritual "improvement" of his situation. When he does manage to escape, a north-north-east wind blows him down the African coast, away from Sallee but also away from Europe: "my resolutions were," he says, "blow which way it would, I would be gone from the horrid place where I was, and leave the rest to Fate" (pp. 19–23). His own power of choice, which had misled him initially when exercised in disregard of, and in conflict with, his providentially ordered role, is thus overruled and supplanted by the force of circumstances. Nor has he the merit in this instance of deferring to the superior will of Providence; on the contrary, he recognizes no higher power at work than "Fate." [16] As he later reflects on his ensuing adventures: "When I was on the desperate

[16] That "Fate" and "Providence" had quite distinct connotations for Defoe is illustrated by a passage in the second Book of *Jure Divino*. Forced to use "Fate" for the sake of a rhyme, he is careful to point out in a note, "A word us'd as expressive of Providence, but not to lessen Providence, or suggest an independent thing, call'd Fate or Fortune, as the

expedition on the desert shores of Africa, I never had
so much as one thought of what would become of me;
or one wish to God to direct me whither I should go,
or to keep me from the danger which apparently
surrounded me, as well from voracious creatures as
cruel savages. But I was merely thoughtless of a God
or a Providence; acted like a mere brute from the
principles of Nature, and by the dictates of common
sense only, and indeed hardly that" (p. 97). Having
cast off the submission he owes to paternal and divine
authority, he finds no real freedom in its place. Not
only in the period of literal slavery, but throughout
these wanderings, he is mastered by events rather than
master of them.

What might appear to be exceptions to this pattern
tend only to confirm it. Crusoe may be said to exercise
choice when he reembarks from London after the first
shipwreck in Yarmouth Roads; when he sets up as a
Brazilian planter rather than returning to England; and
when he decides to undertake the slaving voyage. But
each of these decisions only deepens the guilt of his
original mischoice. They do this first by repeating and
confirming the substance of the original sin—that is,
by obeying unruly inclination rather than reason and

Heathen Determin'd it" (*Jure Divino*, octavo edition
[1706], p. 22). And in the *Serious Reflections* he speaks of
"the notions of decree, destiny, fate, or whatever we weakly
call Providence" (p. 182; cf. also pp. 202–03). Thus when
Crusoe is made to speak of "fate," as here and at p. 14, he is
probably meant to appear culpable. Cf. Richard Whitlock,
*ZOOTOMIA, Or, Observations on the Present Manners of
the English: Briefly Anatomizing the Living by the Dead*
(1654), p. 423 (quoting Lipsius); Richard Blackmore, *Creation*, Book v, 2nd edition (1712), pp. 223–26; Samuel Clarke,
Sermons on Several Subjects, 7th edition, 12 vols. (1744), VI,
192, 195.

duty, and thus drawing what might have seemed a momentary lapse into a settled habit of conduct; and, second, by adding further dimensions to the original sin, for to headstrong obstinacy is added an itch for gain and a desire of "rising faster than the nature of the thing admitted." Rather than indicating the power of choice on Crusoe's part, these "decisions" thus mark the further enslavement of his will. When, for instance, he undertakes the slaving venture, he says "I was hurried on, and obeyed blindly the dictates of my fancy rather than my reason" (p. 43). By this time there really is an element of fatality in his actions, and his situation approaches that described by Tillotson in a sermon "Of the Deceitfulness and Danger of Sin": "when men have brought themselves to this pass, they are almost under a fatal necessity of sinning on. I do not believe that God hath absolutely predestinated any man to ruin, but by a long course of wilful sin men may in a sort predestinate themselves to it, and chuse wickedness so long till it almost becomes necessary, and till they have brought themselves under all imaginable disadvantage of contributing any thing towards their own recovery." [17] The role of habit in hardening the sinner, and depriving him of the very power to see, much less choose, what is good, will be examined in more detail in the next chapter. Here the process is noted merely as another feature of Crusoe's wanderings that shows his worsening spiritual predicament.

[17] *Works of the Most Reverend Dr. John Tillotson*, 12th edition, 10 vols. (Dublin, 1739), 1, 209–10; cf. Edward Waple, *Thirty Sermons Preached on Several Occasions* (1714), pp. 94–95; *Unum Necessarium, or The Doctrine and Practice of Repentance*, in *The Whole Works of the Right Reverend Jeremy Taylor*, edited by Reginald Heber, rev. by Charles P. Eden, 10 vols. (1847–1854), VII, 166–68.

A third and most important characteristic of these wanderings is that Crusoe neglects or actively flouts each opportunity to reverse his course. In addition to the relinquishment, first of rational choice, then gradually of any effective control over the course of events, his progress in sin is marked by a growing obtuseness towards Providential threats and deliverances. He goes on in his willful truancy despite invitations, both gentle and harsh, to mend his ways. The various natural phenomena that affect his outward career so drastically can be regarded as making up a regular series of such invitations, and indeed Crusoe himself comes to see them in this light at the time of his conversion.

That God brings about tempests, earthquakes, and other apparent deviations from the even tenor of things was a natural corollary of the doctrine of Providence; nor was it inconsistent with "scientific" explanations of meteors, eclipses, and epidemics to attribute them to God. Through a distinction between first and second causes, this belief managed to hold its own long after rational explanations were available, and the phenomena themselves had ceased to be objects of merely superstitious awe. Equally widespread and enduring was the belief that such phenomena, whatever their scientific explanations, are more or less explicit statements of God's intention towards those affected. With so many Biblical precedents for the divine punishment of cities or nations, it is not surprising that the three major public calamities of Defoe's lifetime—the plague of 1665, the fire of 1666, and the storm of 1703—were generally interpreted as tokens of God's wrath towards English sins. But readers have often been disturbed by the extension of this doctrine to cases involving single individuals. The supposition that one man could provoke God to stir up the elements for his personal warning or correction has struck many critics as sheer fanaticism. As noted in Chapter I, nineteenth- and twentieth-century editors are consistently exasperated by what they regard as the grotesque self-importance of spiritual autobiographers in such circumstances, and critics of Defoe have been equally prompt to label this belief, expressed at various points in his works, one of his traits of residual Puritan enthusiasm.[18]

But it did not seem so to Defoe's contemporaries. In the writings of Anglicans and Dissenters alike, man is exhorted to observe, interpret, and heed all such phenomena as declarations of the divine will. In any given storm or epidemic, the individual will be either one of the sufferers or one of those spared: in either case he is

[18] Thomas Heywood, who edited the *Diary of the Rev. Henry Newcome* for the Chetham Society in 1849, has this to say about the egocentric folly of making a personal "improvement" of events: "The barefaced impostures of the Roman soothsayer, who could see in all that passed around him what the Deity meant to be interpreted to man, hardly provoke more pity than the self-delusion which prompted Newcome to read in all events a hint for himself, and generally, sanctioning the course most to his own liking. This was one of the objectionable superstitions to which the Puritans were inclined, and is well described by Lord Bacon as 'taking an aim at Divine matters by human, which cannot but breed mixture of imaginations'" (Introduction, pp. xi–xii). As we have seen, of course, Newcome did have his fellows in this habit, nor were they Puritans alone; yet Heywood's remarks are a fair specimen of the modern attitude towards this "objectionable superstition." Similar charges against Defoe are to be found in Paul Dottin, *Daniel De Foe et ses Romans* (Paris, 1924), pp. 354–55, 536; James Sutherland's *Defoe* (1937), p. 14, repeats the substance of these charges, though in a more moderate tone.

obliged to scrutinize the event for its significance to
him personally. As afflictions, such events were often
discussed in terms of the text, "Know ye the rod, and
who hath appointed it" (Micah 6:9). In a sermon
delivered at Dr. Annesley's Cripplegate Exercises, the
well-known Dissenter William Bates deplores the failure to do so as "a prodigious despising of God's
hand"; [19] and John Ryther imputes this fault more
particularly to mariners who disregard storms. They
are deaf, he says, to the calls of Providence: "God
speaks to them once, yea twice, by his judgments as
well as his mercies, but they regard him not. They are
called upon to 'hear the voice of the rod, and him that
hath appointed it,' but they are 'like the deaf adder';
nothing makes them hear or feel. Afflictions are lost
upon them. The storm does not awaken them." [20] In
neglecting to read a meaning for himself in storms at
sea, the sailor effectively frustrates the divine purpose
in sending them. It is only gradually, however, that he
acquires this callousness: at first he tends to be alarmed,
and to form good resolutions, but after weathering a

[19] *Cripplegate Exercises*, II, 589; on this text, see Samuel
Slater, *Cripplegate Exercises*, III, 328; John Owen, "Of Spiritual Mindeness" (1681), in *Works*, edited by William H.
Goold, 24 vols. (1850–1855), VII, 308. On affliction as a call to
repentance, cf. also Digby Cotes, "The Advantage of Afflictions," in *Fifteen Sermons Preach'd on Several Occasions*
(Oxford, 1721), esp. pp. 99–100.

[20] *A Plat for Mariners*, p. 31. In *A Sermon Preach'd . . .
For the late Dreadful Storm* (1704), p. 21, T[imothy]
C[ruso] argues that we should "so improve such Visitations,
that when others are gone to Heaven in a Storm, we may not
go down in our Calm to an infernal Tempest." Cf. Defoe's
treatment of the same event in *The Storm: Or, A Collection
of the most Remarkable Casualties and Disasters Which
happen'd in the Late Dreadful Tempest, Both by Sea and
Land* (1704).

few storms his terror wears off, and boldness, or even bravado, takes its place. Preachers very frequently dwelt on this process because it furnished such a neat paradigm for the course of sinners in general. It appears not only in sermons addressed to seamen, where we should expect to find it, but as a commonplace of seventeenth-century religious literature.[21] That Crusoe himself undergoes this process has been suggested earlier, and will be shown in more detail. Once again, motifs employed constantly in spiritual autobiographies and practical works for their illustrative or metaphorical value are woven into the actual, outward narrative of *Robinson Crusoe*, yet seem to retain their conventional significance.

A related point about Crusoe's afflictions arises from the very fact that they all have to do more or less directly with the sea. In stressing the idea that every calamity contains a Providential lesson for those affected by it, preachers often maintained that the specific nature of the visitation will suggest its import, through some link with what is amiss. In the words of one divine, "whatever particular proportion or correspondence you may observe between this or that circumstance in your affliction and your former transgressions, be especially careful to act according to that

[21] A typical specimen of this nautical image may be found in Joseph Caryl's *Exposition with Practical Observations upon the Book of Job*, 2 vols. (1676–1677), I, col. 763: "The third step [in the degrees of hardness] is, custom in sinning. It argues great boldness to venture often. One said of him that escaped danger at sea, if you go again, you have no reason to complain, though you be wrack'd. Mariners are fearful of storms at first, but through custom they play with them. When a man comes off once safe from sin, he will venture again, and so often, till at last he thinks there is scarce any venture in sin. He grows bold and hardy."

more peculiar and express voice of the rod." [22] An interesting analogy was used to enforce this argument. Thomas Manton, an influential Dissenter, says that "When the sin is written upon the judgment, and there are some remarkable circumstances wherein the sin and the judgment meet . . . God's retaliation is very notable. Many judgments have a signature upon them, as many herbs in nature have a signature to show for what use they serve." [23] Among Manton's Anglican contemporaries, John Tillotson uses the same image in a sermon on "The bad and the good Use of God's signal Judgments upon others": "the hand of God doth sometimes as it were by a finger point at the sin, which it designs to punish: as . . . when a sin is punish'd in its own kind, with a judgment so plainly suited to it, and so pat, that the punishment carries the very mark and signature of the sin upon it." [24] Angli-

---

[22] Philip Doddridge, *The Rise and Progress of Religion in the Soul* (1745), p. 367; cf. p. 238. The principle had been stated a century earlier by Richard Sibbes in *The Soul's Conflict with Itself, and Victory over Itself by Faith* (1635), in *Complete Works*, ed. Alexander B. Grosart, 7 vols. (Edinburgh, 1862), I, 211. For a fuller discussion, see also Jeremy Taylor's sermon, "Apples of Sodom; or the Fruits of Sin," in his *Works*, IV, 263, 270.

[23] Sermon on Psalm 119:118, in *The Complete Works of Thomas Manton, D.D.*, 9 vols. (1870–1872), II, 535–36; cf. Timothy Cruso, *The Mighty Wonders of a Merciful Providence* (1689), p. 11. The second meaning of "signature" given in Johnson's dictionary is "A mark upon any matter, particularly upon plants, by which their nature or medicinal use is pointed out."

[24] *Works*, X, 271–72. Defoe was always fond of this idea. He saw it as no mere coincidence that some Tories who had toasted King William's horse were themselves fatally thrown: see *The Mock-Mourners* (1702), and especially *Review*, VI, 368. In various cases he maintained that "We may read our Sin in our Punishment": cf. *The Family Instructor*, I, 285; II,

can and Dissenter thus agree that an event may, like an herb, bear outward marks of its meaning or function. This is noteworthy in itself, as further evidence of the tendency to regard all objects and events as having a significance, whether obvious or latent, which man must extract from them. But it has particular bearing on Crusoe's own afflictions. His main impulse in running away is towards the sea itself, rather than any ulterior economic or geographic goal; to him the sea is sufficient attraction, and not the route to any destination, or even the setting for any career. By the same token, the sea turns out to be more than the mere scene of his afflictions. The Captain of the ship that founders in Yarmouth Roads interprets Crusoe's first sea venture for him: " 'Young man,' says he, 'you ought never to go to sea any more, you ought to take this for a plain and visible token, that you are not to be a seafaring man.' " [25] He goes on, in fact, to make quite explicit the comparison between Crusoe and Jonah. The result is that the sea, the very object of Crusoe's infatuation, becomes the Providential agent of his chastisement. So it is especially revealing that the sea should prove so hostile to him: his tribulations seem to have "the very mark and signature" of his sins upon them, and his

---

219; *More Reformation. A Satyr upon Himself. By the Author of The True Born English-Man* (1703), sig. [A3ʳ]; *Religious Courtship*, p. 185; *Review*, III, 103; *Applebee's Journal*, April 28, 1722, in William Lee, *Daniel Defoe: His Life and Recently Discovered Writings*, 3 vols. (1869), II, 516.

[25] *Robinson Crusoe*, p. 14. Later, speaking of his decision to undertake the slaving voyage, Crusoe says he ought not to have "gone upon a voyage to sea, attended with all its common hazards, to say nothing of the reasons I had to expect particular misfortunes to myself" (p. 43). See also *Serious Reflections*, p. 197.

failure to grasp this at the time serves as a further indication of his blind willfulness.

In certain cases, of course, tempests and similar phenomena might operate as deliverances rather than afflictions. When a city or nation escapes a doom threatening to overwhelm it, or when an individual is spared the common effects of fire, plague, or other general calamities, Providence is again responsible. Indeed, afflictions and deliverances are regarded as having essentially the same purpose, so that sermons of humiliation and thanksgiving tend to be strikingly similar in argument if not in tone. In other words, God's dealings with man may vary outwardly, but they are uniform in intent.[26] Two special features of Providential deliverances should be noted, however. First there is the fact that deliverances at sea were seen as particularly dramatic and convincing instances of the role of Providence, so that these nautical motifs occur in religious works of all kinds. Following

[26] Writing on the fire of 1666, one divine expresses this idea in the following way: "God prosecutes the same design both in the severe and in the more gentle dispensations of his Providence. He labours to reclaim a perverse and crooked generation, and omits no kind of method proper to effect it. When he threatens us, he admonishes us of our duty and danger; when he chastens us, he calls our Sins to remembrance, he admonisheth us to amend our ways, and put away the evil of our doings: when he removes his rod, and again exercises patience and longsuffering towards us, he vouchsafes to make a farther experiment, what effect goodness will have upon us, and whether it will (at least after severity) lead us to repentance." (William Hopkins, *A Sermon Preached . . . September 3, 1683*, p. 13.) These remarks are typical, and obviously can be applied to somber or joyful occasions alike, to sermons on the disasters of 1665 and 1666 or on the anniversary of the Gunpowder Plot and William III's landing.

David's declaration in Psalm 107 that God's workings are remarkably clear in the case of those who "go down to the sea in ships, and occupy their business in great waters," preachers and poets alike drew heavily on seafaring for Providential exempla. It is true that Newtonian astronomy supplied new illustrations of the extent of general Providence, ordering and sustaining the universe as a whole. But the benevolent operation of particular Providence continued to be shown through traditional images, such as these maritime ones. In his poem on Providence, for instance, John Pomfret says,

> Let the poor Ship-wreck'd Saylor show,
> To what invisible protecting Pow'r
> He did his Life and Safety owe,
> When the loud Storm his well-built Vessel tore,
> And half a shatter'd Plank convey'd him to the Shore.[27]

Passages similar to this one were quoted earlier; they are very common, and are mentioned here only to stress again that the intimate association between the doctrine of Providence and the incidents of seafaring occurs not only in homiletic and practical works, but is characteristic of imaginative literature in general at this period.

Another important feature of these Providential deliverances is summed up in a text frequently

---

[27] "Providence" from "Upon the Divine Attributes. A Pindaric Essay," in *Poems upon Several Occasions*, 4th edition (1716), p. 109. Compare *The Spectator*, No. 489, where Psalm 107 is briefly considered as a specimen of the sublime, followed by Addison's "divine ode" ("How are Thy servants blest, O Lord").

preached upon, "Call upon me in the day of trouble, and I will deliver thee, and thou shalt glorify me" (Psalm 50:15). We have seen that afflictions, far from being the result of accident or chance, are brought about by God to reclaim sinners, and that deliverances have the same cause and purpose. But deliverances have the further function of making man acknowledge his dependence on God for all goods. They demonstrate to him, in an especially forcible way, that not only his welfare, but his bare preservation, is a gift for which he should be thankful.[28]

Bearing these ideas in mind, we may return to the problem of interpreting Crusoe's own career. From the time he first embarks at Hull, he undergoes a varied sequence of afflictions and deliverances; although each does contribute to the action by bringing him a step nearer the island, his "strange surprising adventures" are of a conventional kind, and help to chart the stages of his inward condition. That they have this latter function is indicated not only by the spiritual significance traditionally attached to such happenings, but more explicitly by Crusoe's own comments. Although he fully comprehends these events only after conversion, there are some guides to their meaning even as they take place: in the course of the storm off Yarmouth, he twice likens himself to the Prodigal Son, the Captain compares him to Jonah, and the action itself resembles the Biblical stories at several points. By what I have called a kind of allusive shorthand, Defoe

[28] This argument is developed at length by John Flavel in *The Seaman's Companion*, in his *Whole Works*, II, 262; cf. his *Divine Conduct*, *Whole Works*, II, 113. See also Sir Matthew Hale's *Contemplations Moral and Divine* (1711; 1st edition, 1676), pp. 423–24.

manages to suggest the spiritual connotations of Crusoe's actions. But other forms of explicit commentary
are to be found prior to his conversion.

When he sets out from Brazil on his slaving venture,
for instance, Crusoe carefully notes that "I went on
board in an evil hour . . . being the same day eight
year that I went from my father and mother at Hull, in
order to act the rebel to their authority, and the fool to
my own interest." Only after his conversion, to be
sure, does he calculate in detail the "strange concur-
rence of days in the various providences that befell
me," and the full significance of this phenomenon is
elaborated only in the *Serious Reflections*.[29] Yet even
at this point in the narrative, although the modern
reader is unlikely to share Defoe's attitude towards
such coincidences, the very assertion of this link between the two embarkations suggests their substantive
affinity; and since the spiritual implications of the first
are already fairly clear, the reader is left in little doubt
as to the meaning of the second. This, then, is another
device by which Defoe is able to comment on the
action and at the same time to establish thematic coherence between outwardly dissimilar episodes.

Nevertheless, the most effective commentary in this
portion of the book probably is furnished not by what
Crusoe says but precisely by what he fails to say. We
have seen how divines of the period regarded such
afflictions and deliverances, and how actual survivors
of shipwrecks and escapees from slavery "improved"
their experiences; indeed, we find Crusoe himself
reflecting on these incidents after his conversion in the

[29] *Robinson Crusoe*, pp. 43, 147; *Serious Reflections*, pp.
189–90.

very manner that so many divines prescribed and so many seafarers practiced. The point is that at the time he undergoes them, they provoke no such reflections. He goes heedlessly on, at first unwilling and gradually unable to perceive the Providential import of his vicissitudes. Their function in the book, then, is not merely to bring him plausibly to an island off the mouth of the Orinoco, but more basically to reveal his increasing obduracy and obtuseness.

I have spoken of several gradual processes in this portion of the book—gradual alienation from God, gradual loss of control over events, gradual hardening—and it is worth looking more closely at their progressive or cumulative character. What happens is that Crusoe reaches his lowest spiritual ebb not at the time of committing his "original sin" but just before conversion. It may seem paradoxical to maintain that he embodies a conventional progression in sin. What new sins does he commit? Is not his sense of sin (when it does emerge) in excess of the actual number and enormity of his misdeeds? Part of an answer to such questions has been suggested already: if he does not repeat his dramatic violation of the fifth commandment, or learn to break any of the latter five, he nevertheless does in effect flout the first more and more boldly. It is true, in other words, that he does not sin against the paternal or social order after first running away, but his defiance of divine order becomes a settled pattern of action. Writers on habitual sin maintained not only that one sin tends to lead to other and greater sins unless repentance intervenes, but also that failure to repent for a past sin is equivalent, in terms of the welfare of one's soul, to the actual commission of new sins.[30] Thus even if each rejection of a Providential call to conversion did not constitute a new sin, Crusoe's later sense of sinfulness would be justified by his prolonged failure to repent of the single, initial sin. In fact, however, he is culpable on both counts, for divines were emphatic in condemning what one of them calls "a daring contradiction to Providence, or a bold venturing on in sin, notwithstanding the vertual-wooings and warning-knocks of Providence to the contrary." [31] The "bold venturing on" not only allows past sin to take firmer hold, but is sinful in itself, so that the guilt is compounded.

Turning to the actual details of this process in Crusoe's case, we may begin by recalling the resemblance to Balaam mentioned earlier. Like Crusoe, Balaam ventures forth on a mission contrary to his clear duty; like Crusoe, his way is opposed by God, but he is blind to the cause of the obstacles, and persists obstinately on his course. As with Crusoe, only the appearance of an angel, brandishing a sword and threatening his destruction, finally forces him to repent. What I wish to draw attention to here is not the outward similarity between, for instance, the two visions of armed, avenging angels, but the inward affinity between the spiritual plights of Balaam and Crusoe. In each case journeying bodily is a graphic representation of erring spiritually; in both cases the ways of sin are repeatedly obstructed, and ultimately blocked al-

[30] See Jeremy Taylor, *Unum Necessarium*, in his *Works*, VII, 152, 159–60; cf. also Defoe, *Due Preparations for the Plague*, p. 144.
[31] T[homas] C[rane], *Isagoge . . .* , pp. 507–08; cf. Andrew Trebeck, *Sermons on Several Occasions* (1713), p. 113.

together, in order to deflect the culprit from his false object and restore him to the true path.

Various Biblical and classical analogues to this process were available to preachers of the period. Obadiah Sedgwick says that God sometimes tries to reclaim erring man *"by a most perfect beleagring* (as it were) *of a projecting sinner:* hedging up all his ways with thorns, or immuring him as in a Castle, and shutting of him up, that there shall be no going out or coming in." [32] Seen in these terms, Crusoe's arrival on the island marks yet another more drastic stage in God's efforts to reclaim him. It is at once the most dramatic of his long series of deliverances, and the most effective barrier to his persistent vagabondage. The shipwreck is meant to halt his erring career and to awaken him to a new life; what happens, however, is that only his outward circumstances change. Initially, to be sure, he is struck by his escape, but his elation soon gives way to despair, for, as he records in his journal, "instead of being thankful to God for my deliverance . . . I ran about the shore, wringing my hands, and beating my head and face, exclaiming at my misery, and crying out, I was undone, undone" (p. 75). When he does regain his composure, he once again fails to interpret the personal significance of what he has just experienced.

On the one hand, the brief ecstasy, as he later calls it, "ended where it began, in a mere common flight of joy," without leading to any "reflection upon the

---

[32] *Parable of the Prodigal*, p. 64; cf. Hosea 2:6, "Therefore, behold, I will hedge up thy way with thorns, and make a wall, that she shall not find her paths." Cf. also Ryther, *Plat for Mariners*, pp. 30–31; [Richard Allestree], *The Causes of The Decay of Christian Piety* (1677), p. 180.

distinguished goodness of the hand which had preserved me," or any "inquiry why Providence had been
thus merciful to me." On the other hand, he later
acknowledges that as soon as he saw he was not
doomed to starve, "all the sense of my affliction wore
off . . . [I] was far enough from being afflicted at
my condition, as a judgment from heaven, or as the
hand of God against me" (p. 98). Regarded *either* as a
deliverance or as an affliction, this episode might have
taken effect, but in fact the Providential design in it is
frustrated, and it takes its place among the calls to
repentance which go unheeded. In terms of Crusoe's
spiritual state, it marks yet another slight of the
"vertual-wooings and warning-knocks of Providence"; like Balaam, he goes mulishly on, although "by
a most perfect beleagring (as it were)" the way of the
"projecting sinner" is now hedged up with thorns.
Thus the arrival at the island may be less of a turning
point than is generally supposed: a new beginning in
only a qualified sense, it is more basically an extension
of a pattern of action initiated by the embarkation at
Hull.

Two important episodes between Crusoe's landing
on the island and his conversion are discussed in the
Appendix—namely the springing up of the barley, and
the earthquake (see pp. 194–96, below). In light of the
foregoing discussion, it should be clear why Crusoe
later singles out these two incidents, among all those
between his landing and his sickness, for special regret-
ful comment. Like the events just considered, they
again display Providence's concern for him and power
over him; they again invite him (once gently, once
harshly) to repent; but they again fail to take effect.
Rather than dwelling further here on their

significance, we shall find it more fruitful to turn directly to the climactic episode of this long series: Crusoe's illness.

It was of course traditional to represent spiritual infirmity through bodily disease, to express God's cure of souls in medical metaphors, and to regard actual sickness as a particularly opportune occasion for setting repentance in motion.[33] Seen against such a background, Crusoe's malady is another striking instance of Defoe's ability to exploit fully the narrative possibilities of commonplace events, and at the same time to avail himself of their conventional spiritual significance. Thus the chart of Crusoe's case history, which he is made to record in his journal (pp. 95–96), has a thoroughly clinical verisimilitude; this gives the dream and its consequences a plausibility which they might have lacked had they come, for instance, in a season of callous, bustling prosperity. More fundamentally, however, Crusoe's sickness and dream serve as final indications of the spiritual condition which he has reached, and of the greatness of the change he is about to undergo. These effects are achieved partly, as already noted, by the overt resemblance between this stern apparition and certain Biblical ones. But they are also owing in part to the tradition of hardy sinners bowed by sickness. Without recapitulating earlier discussion of such motifs in spiritual autobiographies, or citing any further evidence of their prevalence in homiletic and practical works, we may recall that they

[33] The first two ideas are elaborated by William Hopkins in *A Sermon Preached . . . September 3, 1683*, pp. 15–16; for the third, see Philip Doddridge, *Practical Discourse of Regeneration*, in *Works*, 10 vols. (Leeds, 1803), I, 507; Tillotson, "Of the End of Judgments, and the Reason of their Continuance," in *Works*, I, 192, 194.

appear very early in the literature of conversion. As one of Defoe's contemporaries obligingly pointed out to his parishioners, "not only by outward Means, but by immediate Operations and Impressions, and those, very sensible, strong, and lively, have the Convictions of some Men been wrought in them. Of all which, St. *Austin* is a most remarkable Instance, who in his *Confessions* (a Book I think translated into English and worthy your Perusal) hath recorded the many Warnings he had from God, by his own Sickness; the Death of his Companions in Sin; the overruling Providences of God; the inward Motions, and Convictions of his own Conscience; and at last by a *Voice* from Heaven; commanding him to take up the Bible, and read." [34]

The preceding examination of Crusoe's adventures after embarking at Hull has shown that besides merely leading him to the island by plausible stages, they function as "the many Warnings" which he, like Augustine, "had from God," and that their sequence is completed not with the arrival at the island but at the point of conversion. The fact that nothing less drastic than the appearance of an avenging angel will serve to awaken Crusoe indicates how grave his spiritual malady has become, yet at the same time enhances the importance of his conversion and heightens the attainments possible to him through regeneration. Earlier chapters have discussed the trait, so common to spiritual autobiographers, of magnifying one's ultimate condition by contrasting it with what preceded conversion. Regarded in these terms, Crusoe's vicissitudes magnify the scope, the patience, and the benevolence of Providence; his conversion, however, magnifies not

[34] Waple, *Thirty Sermons*, p. 395.

only the abundance of grace to the sinner, but also, by implication, the potential stature of the ex-sinner himself. It was said of the Puritan worthy Robert Bolton that "it pleased God to bring him to repentance, but by such a way as the Lord seldom useth, but upon such strong vessels, as he intendeth for strong encounters, and rare employments; for the Lord ranne upon him as a Giant, taking him by the neck, and shaking him to pieces, as he did *Iob;* beating him to the ground as he did *Paul,* by laying before him the ugly visage of his sins, which lay so heavy upon him that he roared for anguish of heart." [35] It is in this tradition that Defoe places Crusoe, by investing his conversion with such grand agents as a fire-clad, spear-brandishing apparition. The section that follows will examine the conversion itself, and Crusoe's subsequent fortunes, in order to establish whether, and in what sense, he is a strong vessel intended for strong encounters and rare employments.

3. CONVERSION AND REGENERATION

In one of his essays, Lord Clarendon says of repentance that "It is almost the only point of faith upon which there is no controversy." [36] Moreover the concept was a fairly simple one, definable in a sentence or two. [37] But despite the clear and uncontroversial

[35] Samuel Clarke, *The Marrow of Ecclesiastical History*, 2nd edition (1654), p. 925.

[36] *Essays, Moral and Entertaining*, 2 vols. (Oxford, 1815), I, 159.

[37] Defoe's definition of repentance in *The Family Instructor* may be regarded as standard: "Repentance is a hearty Sorrow for your Sins already past, and solemn, serious Resolutions, to commit no more; and this Sorrow must proceed not only from a Fear of eternal Punishment, but from a

nature of the doctrine, the process by which one actually came to repent might be quite complex: in fact, there was a regular progression through which autobiographers and other writers on repentance usually led their readers. First there was the provocation to repentance—the event or impression which set the whole process in motion; next there was reflection or consideration, a "coming to oneself"; this was followed by "conviction" or "godly sorrow," a phase of remorseful self-accusation; then there came the stage, to which most writers reserved the term "conversion," when God actually relieved and reclaimed the sufferer. Each of the stages could vary considerably in form and intensity, but their sequence was fairly constant, and we find Crusoe passing through them in the traditional manner.

At the end of the preceding section it was noted that the vision of the avenging angel which precipitates Crusoe's repentance, however fanciful it may seem, has various precedents. As one of Bishop Hall's *Soliloquies*, on "God's Various Proceedings," points out, the ways of initiating the process are infinite:

"What strange varieties do I find in the workings of God with man! one, where I find him gently and

---

Hatred of Sin, for its own evil Nature, and as it is offensive to the Holiness of God" (I, 188; cf. also II, 321). The Westminster Assembly's *Confession of Faith* declares of repentance that "By it, a Sinner, out of the sight and sense, not onely of the danger, but also of the filthinesse and odiousnesse of his sinnes, as contrary to the holy nature, and righteous law of God; and, upon the apprehension of his mercy in Christ to such as are penitent, so grievs for, and hates his sins, as to turne from them all unto God, purposing and endeavouring to walk with him in all the wayes of his Commandments" (2nd edition [1658], pp. 50–51).

plausibly inviting men to their conversion; another, where I find him frighting some others to heaven: some, he trains up in a goodly education, and, without any eminent change, calls them forth to an exemplary profession of his name; some others, he chooseth out of a life notoriously lewd to be the great patterns of a sudden reformation: one, that was only formal in his devotion, without any true life of grace, is, upon a grievous sickness, brought to a lively sense of godliness; . . . another, that was cast down with a sad despair of God's mercy, is raised up by the fall of an unbroken glass, or by some comfortable dream, or by the seasonable word of a cheerful friend: one is called at the sixth hour; another, not till the eleventh: one, by fair and probable means; another, by contraries; so as even the work of Satan himself hath been made the occasion of the conversion of his soul." [38]

In Crusoe's case it is a dream, but scarcely a "comfortable" one, that effectually bestirs him. Unlike his previous alarms, which had soon subsided, this one provokes him to review his past career: "conscience," he says, "that had slept so long, began to awake, and I began to reproach myself with my past life" (p. 99). He now reflects on the various Providential chastisements and deliverances which he had neglected or dismissed. In doing so, he becomes keenly aware of his spiritual plight, and thus moves a step closer to repentance. His reflections at this stage make up what writers on the subject generally refer to as "consideration"; [39] this typically merges into "conviction," and

[38] *Works*, VIII, 72–73; cf. William Turner, *A Compleat History . . .* , p. 83.

[39] For a discussion of "consideration," with an extended specimen of the way it was to be conducted, see Sedgwick,

such in the case with Crusoe. He reports that amid the "dreadful reproaches of my conscience, . . . My thoughts were confused, the convictions great upon my mind, and the horror of dying in such a miserable condition, raised vapours into my head with the mere apprehensions" (p. 99). Such sorrows and fears commonly mark this phase of the process, for, as one writer observes, "The work of Regeneration or the New Birth cannot be wrought without many pangs or throwes, nor does God ever almost bring a bad man to become a good one without some trouble and disorder of Mind." [40] Indeed, Crusoe's state borders on despair; his oppressive reflections, he says, "extorted some words from me, like praying to God, though I cannot say they were either a prayer attended with desires or with hopes; it was rather the voice of mere fright and distress" (p. 99). And in the depths of his depression he finds himself facing "difficulties to struggle with, too great for even Nature itself to support, and no assistance, no help, no comfort, no advice" (p. 100). Our analyses of Fraser's *Memoirs* and the *Account* have shown how the opening phases of repentance tend to reduce the penitent to a low ebb of despondency, in which he feels altogether helpless and abandoned; only when he has acknowledged his own utter insufficiency and worthlessness is he in a posture to receive forgiveness and relief. This also is true of

Parable of the Prodigal, pp. 69–70; cf. also the chapter "Of Consideration" in Goodman, *The Penitent Pardoned*, p. 136f.; Wright, *Being Born Again* . . . , p. 90. All three writers base their remarks on Luke 15:17, "And when he came to himself . . ."

[40] Payne, *A Practical Discourse of Repentance*, p. 289; cf. Ezekiel Hopkins on "The Nature and Necessity of Regeneration: or the New-Birth." in *Works*, p. 534.

Crusoe. Having voiced the lament just quoted, he cries out, "Lord, be my help, for I am in great distress." This, "the first prayer, if I may call it so, that I had made for many years," signals the submission which the long series of vicissitudes considered in the preceding section had been designed, but had failed, to bring about.

Crusoe's "convictions," however, do not in themselves constitute repentance, for although godly sorrow was seen as an essential stage or component of repentance, it makes up only a part of the total process.[41] As shown earlier, it was believed that once man had been brought to contrite humility, God had to interpose if the matter was not to end in total despair. Actual conversion, in other words, was regarded as a gift which man can and must make himself eligible to receive, but which he cannot command or obtain by his own efforts. Crusoe's convictions, culminating in his first brief prayer, render him fit for the help he implores; as with the father in the parable, God's grace goes out to meet and reclaim the returning prodigal. It is interesting to observe that Defoe employs external detail, at this point as elsewhere, to indicate the inward spiritual state of the hero. Just as grave bodily illness parallels the crisis in Crusoe's spiritual malady, so the first stirrings of spiritual renewal are heralded by the signs of physical recovery that appear the day after his

[41] On this matter, see Waple, "Of Repentance: A Sense of Sin," in *Thirty Sermons*, pp. 154-55; Payne, *Practical Discourse of Repentance*, p. 338; and a series of sermons by Charles Wroughton on "The Nature of Repentance: The Danger of delaying it: And the Invalidity of a Death-bed Repentance," in his *Thirteen Sermons, Chiefly on Practical Subjects* (1728), pp. 55-137; cf. especially the distinction between μεταμέλεια and μετάνοια on pp. 57-59.

prayer (p. 100). It seems significant that the sea, too, which has hitherto proved such a consistently hostile and turbulent element in his experience, is on this occasion "very calm and smooth." In any case Crusoe, who is still too weak to walk, sits down on the ground, gazes out to sea, and meditates, with the insight of a fledgling physico-theologist, on the significance of what he sees. Though he lacks as yet the aid of God's Word, he now begins to perceive God through his Works. The implication is that unless one is willfully blind—as indeed Crusoe has been up to his point—it quickly becomes obvious that "God has made all these things," and that "He guides and governs them all," as well, so that "nothing can happen in the great circuit of His works, either without His knowledge or appointment" (p. 101). Crusoe's dawning awareness that all creation, including himself, is subject to the disposition of Providence still does not afford him consolation, however: at this point it merely deepens his sense of folly and guilt in having been so long oblivious of the fact. But such an acknowledgment of God's power, coinciding with Crusoe's bodily weakness in the first stage of convalescence, opens the way to divine relief. Thus "directed by Heaven no doubt," he rummages in one of the salvaged sea-chests, where he finds the Bible and some tobacco, "a cure both for soul and body" (pp. 102–03). Opening the Bible, he reads as the first words those of Psalm 50, "Call upon me in the day of trouble, and I will deliver thee, and thou shalt glorify me." His first response, it is true, is to interpret deliverance as referring to his isolation; of deliverance in this sense, the prospect is so faint that he forms no great hopes. But it soon occurs to him that in poring so much upon deliverance "from the main affliction," he is disregarding the deliverance from sickness he has just received, and before long it further dawns on him that according to "a true sense of things," one "will find deliverance from sin a much greater blessing than deliverance from affliction" (pp. 104–05, 107).

He does not gain this latter realization, however, until after a second encounter with an apposite Biblical text: "I was earnestly begging of God to give me repentance, when it happened providentially, the very day, that reading the Scripture, I came to these words, 'he is exalted a Prince and a Saviour, to give repentance, and to give remission' [Defoe's paraphrase of Acts 5:31]. I threw down the book; and with my heart as well as my hands lifted up to heaven, in a kind of ecstasy of joy, I cried aloud, 'Jesus . . . Thou exalted Prince and Saviour, give me repentance!'

"This was the first time that I could say, in the true sense of the words, that I prayed in all my life; for now I prayed with a sense of my condition, and with a true Scripture view of hope founded on the encouragement of the Word of God; and from this time, I may say, I began to have hope that God would hear me" (p. 106).

If any single episode can be isolated as the book's turning point, it is probably this one. God's threats give way to his promises, and Crusoe's dismal apprehensions are replaced by a hope that grows towards assurance.

Yet it is worth observing that this change, significant as it is, is presented with a minimum of rapture, nor is there any pretense to total, immediate transformation. The reasons for this have already been suggested: reacting in embarrassment against the enthusiastic transports of earlier conversion accounts, spiritual autobiographers of the late seventeenth and early eighteenth centuries tried to avoid the stigma of fanaticism by speaking of the change with careful restraint, by repressing any tendency to revel garrulously in their newfound grace.[42] Thus Crusoe does momentarily experience "a kind of ecstacy of joy," but does not dwell on these emotions; nor to be sure is this elation lasting, although, as Fraser had quietly remarked, "something remained." Moreover, his regeneration is by no means instantaneous. Like the recovery from his ague, it is a gradual regaining of strength. What has come upon

[42] Compare Defoe's account of the process of repentance in *The Family Instructor* (1, 195–96). After narrating the business, he sums it up as follows:

"From the beginning of the wicked Boy's Convictions, *Note,* that Sense of Danger is the first Thing ordinarily that discovers itself in Conviction of Sin, and this leads to enquiring after what we are next to do; as the Jailor who first came in trembling, then asks, *What must I do?* [Acts 16:30]

"When the Boy, after his first Conviction, recollects Things by himself *while his Companion is gone for the Bible,* he is struck with Horror at his Condition, but the Spirit of God working graciously in him, lays the Promise of God, *as it were,* full in his Way, in order to give him Hope, and at the first Appearance of Hope he breaks out vehemently in Prayer; when his Comrade returns, and innocently inquires about what he said, it appears from him, that his Prayer was a kind of Extasy, mov'd by a supernatural Power in his Heart, that affected him in a violent manner, so that he hardly could give an Account of it himself, but says wildly, *he trembled and cry'd out.*

"There are, no doubt, such strong Impressions of the Spirit of God accompanying true Convictions, and the great regenerating Work of Grace in the Heart, as may be inexpressible, even by the Persons themselves, yet far from *Enthusiastick,* or affected; nor are these Impressions to be slighted, much less ridicul'd."

Cf. also the descriptions of repentance in *Religious Courtship,* pp. 60–61, and *Due Preparations,* pp. 137f.

him with suddenness is the grace to repent and the hope of obtaining remission of his sins: the actual work of regeneration is achieved only through a settled change in attitude and behavior, and clearly requires time.

Although this conversion scene is remarkably free from cant about either the sensations or the extent of the change, Defoe nevertheless makes clear that a change of great significance has taken place. Crusoe reflects almost at once that "My condition now began to be, though not less miserable as to my way of living, yet much easier to my mind . . . I had a great deal of comfort within, which, till now, I knew nothing of" (p. 107). In fact, the attainment of a new kind and degree of serenity is one of the most marked characteristics of his latter state. This is not to say, of course, that he is now simply freed from all anxiety. At various points in the subsequent narrative he experiences "frights" and "consternations"; some of them are fully as harrowing as the "strange surprising adventures" that preceded his conversion, and perhaps more so, since he had then been callous towards dangers and deliverances alike. Now, however, he becomes better able to confront new hazards, and to dispel their terrors, for he gains security from the conviction that he is an object of Providential care. In other words, it is not that his belief shields him from further vicissitudes, but that such vicissitudes either fail to discompose him or else agitate him only when he forgets he is under divine protection.[43]

---

[43] Sustained by this belief, Crusoe's condition comes to resemble that described by the pious Dr. Aylet, who exclaims, in Spenserian stanzas of greater doctrinal than poetic merit,

Evidence of this is to be found in Crusoe's discovery of the footprint in the sand. We are given a lively picture of his terrors, both on the beach and during the sleepless night that follows. After recounting them at great length, he confesses "Thus my fear banished all my religious hope. All that former confidence in God, which was founded upon such wonderful experience as I had had of His goodness, now vanished, as if He that had fed me by miracle hitherto could not preserve, by His power, the provision which He had made for me by His goodness" (pp. 172–73). But afterward, "when [he] had a little recovered [his] first surprise," Crusoe again calls to mind the power, wisdom, and bounty of Providence, and thus regains his composure. He reflects that " 'twas my unquestioned duty to resign myself absolutely and entirely to His will; and, on the other hand, it was my duty also to hope in Him,

---

O what inestimable quietness!
From hence ariseth to a godly minde,
Though evils without number him oppress,
Which like so many Deaths he then doth finde,
    Knowing not how his wretched selfe to winde,
From cruelty, which him fast followeth,
And doth so fast with cords and fetters binde,
    That ev'ry minute threateneth his Death;
And scarcely suffers him to draw his languid breath.

    Yet if this Light of *heav'nly Providence*
Shines to his Soule; then all Anxiety,
Feare, Care, Distrust, are banisht quite from thence,
And he releev'd in all extremity:
    Then knows he that one gracious Majesty,
Heer by his power so directeth all,
By wisdom rules, and by his Bonity
Disposeth so, that nothing ever shall,
    But for Gods glory and his own good him befall.

(*Divine, and Moral Speculations in Metrical Numbers, Upon Various Subjects* [1654], p. 435: "Of Providence.")

pray to Him, and quietly to attend the dictates and directions of His daily Providence." [44] And again, when his "cogitations, apprehensions, and reflections" return to disturb him, he recalls the passage from Psalm 50 which had been of such service to him during his sickness, and declares, "Upon this, rising cheerfully out of my bed, my heart was not only comforted, but I was guided and encouraged to pray earnestly to God for deliverance. When I had done praying, I took up my Bible, and opening it to read, the first words that presented to me were, 'Wait on the Lord, and be of good cheer, and He shall strengthen thy heart; wait, I say, on the Lord.' It is impossible to express the comfort this gave me. In answer, I thankfully laid down the book, and was no more sad, at least, not on that occasion." [45]

At other times, too, Crusoe is downcast: his trust in Providence does not exempt him from alarms and dejections, but it reasserts itself so as to rescue him from them. [46] Conversion was not seen as providing immunity to spiritual turmoils, but rather a new strength with which to resolve them, and it is this that Crusoe gains.

[44] P. 174; on these duties, see Wright, *Being Born Again . . .* , p. 121; John Howe, "Of Thoughtfulness for the Morrow" (1681), in *Works*, edited by Henry Rogers, 6 vols. (1862), IV, 108; Tamworth Reresby, *A Miscellany of Ingenious Thoughts and Reflections, In Verse and Prose* (1721), p. 139.

[45] Pp. 174–75; Crusoe quotes Psalm 27:14. At the conclusion of this passage and on at least one other occasion, he also echoes I Sam. 1:18; cf. pp. 146–47.

[46] Cf. p. 194: "after seriously thinking of these things, I should be very melancholy, and sometimes it would last a great while; but I resolved it, at last, all into thankfulness to that Providence which had delivered me from so many unseen dangers, and had kept me from those mischiefs which I could no way have been the agent in delivering myself from."

Whatever its interruptions, then, his attitude becomes one of composure; this composure springs from a mixture of hope and resignation, which in turn is owing to a new awareness of the existence and nature of Providence. His new attitude not only supports him in the various crises which punctuate his later years on the island, as I have just argued, but also largely offsets the painful loneliness of his long isolation. One of the early results of his repentance is that, as he puts it, "I acquiesced in the dispositions of Providence, which I began now to own and to believe ordered everything for the best." [47] Through such acquiescence, he learns to find both consolations for and positive benefits in his solitary state. This aspect of his situation is expressed most forcibly in his series of annual thanksgivings, but it appears on other occasions as well.[48] Indeed, it was a constant theme in preaching of the period that solitude has special compensations for those who realize that they are never out of the presence of God. Thus Edward Waple, drawing on Cicero's *Offices*, argues as follows: "If a wise Heathen could say, that he was never less idle than when he was out of Business; nor

[47] P. 120; cf. Tillotson, "The Wisdom of God in his Providence," in *Works*, VI, 418–19: "the very heathen poet . . . adviseth us to commit all our concernments to [God]. . . . Leave it (says he) to the wiser gods, to consider and determine what is fittest for thee, and most for thy advantage; and though they do not always give thee what thou desirest, and that which pleaseth thee best, yet they will give thee that which is most fit and convenient for thee; for man is more dear to the gods, than he is to himself." Bishop Bull makes the same use of Juvenal's doctrine that *charior est illis homo quam sibi*: see *The Works of George Bull*, edited by E. Burton, 2nd edition, 6 vols. (Oxford, 1846), I, 468.

[48] Pp. 124–26, 142–44; cf. also pp. 185–86, 208. Crusoe's thanksgivings are discussed further in the Appendix, pp. 196–97.

less alone than when he was in Private; . . . How much more can a Christian say so, who believes one Supreme God, and a Providence, and invisible Powers above him, and can look up to Heaven, with Confidence to God, as a Father in Christ; and can lay all his Wants, and his Necessities before him, in assurance of being heard, and relieved by him. O comfortable Retirement! O happy Rest! or may I not rather say, O *blessed Company*, O *busy* and *laborious Rest!*" [49] Crusoe's reactions to his solitude do vary, of course, so that he lapses more than once into extreme melancholy over his condition. Yet on the whole his isolation is made tolerable, and frequently strikes him as a positive blessing. Recognizing his dependence on Providence, he submits to its government and becomes responsive to manifestations of its will concerning him. But its very immediacy is as important to his peace of mind as its power and beneficence, since it is a sense of God's nearness and accessibility that supplies his *"blessed Company."*

Nor is his regeneration confined to the change in belief or attitude. Though the inward alteration is basic, his overt behavior is equally affected, and offers palpable evidence of the change that has taken place within him. In the first place, certain habitual or at least recurrent actions bespeak his altered condition. Hopeful resignation has already been mentioned as a feature of his inward change; it finds tangible expression, however, in his prayers and thanksgivings. Surveys of his activities which take into account all that he builds and grows, all his carpentry and husbandry, his potting and baking, but omit or slight these religious observ-

[49] *Thirty Sermons*, p. 272.

ances, are at best incomplete and at worst seriously distorted. Not only do the latter bulk large in the narrative, but they give the economic activity itself a meaning which it had lacked prior to conversion. As is demonstrated more fully in the Appendix, Crusoe now goes about his tasks in a different spirit, so that both the objects and the results of his labors are conditioned by his prayers and thanksgivings. Through prayer, he seeks and obtains divine guidance and assistance in his efforts; and through ascribing their outcome to Providence, he not only takes new relish in those which succeed, but manages to be undismayed by those which are delayed, botched, or frustrated.

Other practices as well reflect the spiritual transformation that Crusoe undergoes. Although he comes to acquiesce in what Providence determines as his lot, and to depend upon divine support and protection, he is by no means passive; he learns to recognize and heed its warnings and promptings. This attitude leads to what some critics have regarded as a superstitious concern for hints and portents, but within the traditions of belief already discussed, 'Crusoe's keen attention to apparent trivia is not excessive. In a world in which nothing can occur without Providential design, piety alone obliges man to vigilance, and since Providence concerns itself in a direct, personal way with the welfare of the individual, prudence likewise demands watchfulness.[50] An earlier chapter has argued that this double incentive is largely responsible for the thoroughness with which spiritual autobiographers assessed everything that happened to them: besides ob-

[50] On the need for such alertness, see "The Exercise and Progress of a Christian," in *The Works of the Learned Benjamin Whichcote*, 4 vols. (Aberdeen, 1751), I, 359–60.

taining indications of their spiritual condition, they were thus able to satisfy the twin dictates of thankfulness and circumspection.

It is particularly noteworthy that Crusoe should come to act in this way, for it provides a fundamental contrast with his earlier behavior. His initial disobedience, as we have seen, had been both sinful and rash. Now, however, through attending, interpreting, and obeying various manifestations of the divine will towards him, he attains the corresponding virtues of piety and prudence. An example is his reaction to visitors from the outside world, the cannibals and the English crew. On each occasion he is restrained, by secret doubts or admonitions, from encounters that would have been his undoing (pp. 191–95, 279–80); in both cases he pauses to advise "all considering men, whose lives are attended with such extraordinary incidents as mine, or even though not so extraordinary, not to slight such secret intimations of Providence. . . . Let no man despise the secret hints and notices of danger which sometimes are given him when he may think there is no possibility of its being real" (pp. 195, 279). In keeping, then, with the autobiographical conventions discussed earlier, Crusoe has frequent opportunities to ascribe his own preservation to Providence. But in addition, he becomes the agent of Providence in the salvation of others. This role is made quite explicit in the case of the English captain (p. 284), and is an important motif in his dealings with Friday. The point here, however, is that Crusoe's regeneration involves not merely a change in attitude or belief, since his new outlook does affect his actual behavior. If for this reason alone, it seems a mistake to suppose that his religion amounts to no more than a superimposed and dispensable commentary on the action.[51]

Crusoe's relations with Friday deserve particular attention because they supply yet another test of the importance of religious concerns to the book's total structure. Like the running away to sea and various events that follow, Friday's role has been discussed by one recent critic mainly in economic terms. His rescue merely marks "the advent of new manpower"; Crusoe's dealings with him are altogether egocentric; communication between them is strictly utilitarian, so that "A functional silence, broken only by an occasional 'No, Friday,' or an abject 'Yes, Master,' is the golden music of Crusoe's *île joyeuse*."[52]

While it cannot be denied that Friday's arrival results in new planting and building, it is surely an error to regard this as its sole, or even its main implication. We have seen that a constant feature of spiritual autobiographies, and indeed a primary motive in their very composition, is the urge to impart to others the benefits of one's own conversion; we have also noted that the growth of this didactic impulse is a phenomenon recognized and endorsed by writers on regenera-

[51] See Ian Watt, *The Rise of the Novel*, p. 81: "Otherworldly concerns do not provide the essential themes of Defoe's novels: but they do punctuate the narrative with comminatory codas that demonstrate a lifetime of somewhat mechanical practice."

[52] *The Rise of the Novel*, pp. 73, 69. Immediately before alleging this "functional silence," Mr. Watt quotes the following remark of Crusoe's, omitting what I have italicized: "*the conversation which employed the hours between Friday and I was such, as made the three years which we lived there together* perfectly and completely happy, if any such thing as complete happiness can be formed in a sublunary state." "Conversation" is the subject of the sentence: through its omission, Crusoe's meaning is reversed.

tion other than autobiographers. On the one hand, to have experienced conversion oneself was regarded as a necessary qualification for evangelizing, and on the other, it was felt that genuine conversion naturally gives rise to a kind of missionary zeal.[53] It is this aspect of Crusoe's relations with Friday that seems most striking, for after being "called plainly by Providence to save this poor creature's life" (p. 225), Crusoe becomes the Providential agent of his rescue from paganism.

Just as Crusoe had discovered for himself the essentials of Christianity by reading the Bible, contemplating the works of nature, and reflecting on his own experience, so his indoctrination of Friday provides a second demonstration of the simplicity and reasonableness of such belief as is necessary to salvation. Moreover, his guidance of Friday displays the progress of Crusoe's own regeneration, in that he now learns to expound and defend his faith. It is true that he is posed by several of Friday's ingenuous questions, and he acknowledges that "I was but a young doctor, and ill enough qualified for a casuist, or a solver of difficulties. . . . I had, God knows, more sincerity than knowledge in all the methods I took for this poor creature's instruction" (pp. 243, 45). But this confession, too, besides lending plausibility in the same way as do his awkward improvisations in other spheres, is part of the traditional conception of the fledgling spiritual guide. As was shown earlier, the lay convert was encouraged to share his discoveries with others not

[53] In *The Farther Adventures of Robinson Crusoe*, the French priest declares that "true religion is naturally communicative, and he that is once made a Christian will never leave a pagan behind him if he can help it" (p. 145).

only for the good it might do them but for the value it must have to himself. In Chapter I we saw the double function—didactic and autodidactic—ascribed throughout the period to spiritual autobiography in particular, and to the exchange of religious knowledge and experience in general. Here the principle is made quite explicit, in Crusoe's declaration that "in laying things open to him, I really informed and instructed myself in many things that either I did not know, or had not fully considered before, but which occurred naturally to my mind upon my searching into them for the information of this poor savage. And I had more affection in my inquiry after things upon this occasion than ever I felt before; so that whether this poor wild wretch was the better for me or no, I had great reason to be thankful that ever he came to me." [54] In short, communication between Crusoe and Friday is "utilitarian" in a sense quite different from that which Mr. Watt has in mind. It is useful not to one party but to both, and it is useful not so much for the exploitation of new manpower—signs, effective enough at first, would have remained sufficient for that—as for the salvation of one soul and the growth of another.

Besides becoming Friday's spiritual mentor, Crusoe is also his master, and a further point should be made about this aspect of their relationship. Prior to his conversion, Crusoe rebels against divine authority, yet his attempt to become independent results in an actual loss of mastery over himself and his circumstances.

---

[54] P. 245; cf. *The Farther Adventures*, p. 142, where it is said of Will Atkins that "when he comes to talk religion to his wife, he will talk himself effectually into it; for attempting to teach others is sometimes the best way of teaching ourselves."

Eventually, through submitting to God and acknowledging his dependence upon Providence, he in fact acquires a new degree of control over his environment, and over himself as well. In seeking to be a law unto himself, he had lost the power that was properly his; in surrendering to the sovereignty of Providence, he gains extraordinary powers. In any case, it seems legitimate to regard his mastery over Friday in this light, as made possible by his own submission to God, and as a further embodiment of a paradox running throughout the book: that sinful independence results in Crusoe's enslavement, both literal and figurative, while virtuous dependence issues in mastery, again literal and figurative.

The paradox might also be stated in terms of the relation between parent and child. In the early part of the book Crusoe virtually orphans himself through disobedience: in challenging the authority of a father he loses the security of a son. But through humbling himself towards his other Father, and reassuming the dutifulness of a son, Crusoe paradoxically gains parental power himself, since his relations with Friday are in large part those of father to child, as he himself declares (p. 232). Thus the parent-child motif further illustrates the nature and extent of the change that Crusoe undergoes.

Crusoe's encounters with Friday and the other savages raise another interesting issue, which was to be treated fully in the *Serious Reflections*, in chapters on "The Present State of Religion in the World" and "Of the Proportion between the Christian and Pagan World." Crusoe asks himself "why it has pleased God to hide . . . saving knowledge from so many millions of souls, who, if I might judge by this poor savage, would make a much better use of it than we did" (p. 233). This problem perplexed Europe throughout the period, and was to have profound effects on Christian thinking, as explorers continued to bring back reports of heathen races in remote lands. It is worth observing, however, that in *Robinson Crusoe* the question is subsumed in the more pervasive issue of the hero's own relationship to God. What happens is that Crusoe's musings on the matter lead him, as he confesses, "too far to invade the sovereignty of Providence, and as it were arraign the justice of so arbitrary a disposition of things" (p. 233); ultimately the question is not so much resolved by any direct answer as dismissed by a gesture of humble acquiescence on the part of the questioner. It is all very well to be concerned about the fate of "millions of souls," but it is still more important not to jeopardize one's own by questioning, much less challenging, the Providential "disposition of things." [55] It is not that Defoe lacked answers: he had them, as he was to prove abundantly in the *Serious Reflections*. It is rather that Crusoe's responses to the problem—first presumptuous, then proper—are what really matter. Once again Defoe has inserted in the narrative an issue possessing intrinsic interest and importance, which would be explored for its own sake in his other writings but which, in the setting of *Robinson Crusoe*,

[55] It should be noted that Defoe uses the image of the clay and the potter from Jeremiah 18 as his final argument against challenging this Providential order, since his earliest known composition, the poetical "Meditacons" of 1681, contains a Pindaric on this text: see "shall The Clay Say Unto The Potter? &ca," in *The Meditations of Daniel Defoe*, edited by George Harris Healey (Cummington, Mass., 1946), pp. 17–19.

is subordinated to a primary concern with the spiritual development of the hero.

Crusoe's relationship with Friday can be summed up in this way: without denying that Friday's arrival has economic implications, it has other results which are equally prominent in purely narrative terms, and probably more significant in thematic terms. Nor is it merely a matter of Crusoe "carrying on a little missionary activity as a sideline," as Basil Willey maintains.[56] Far from being a sideline, such activity is a crucial feature of Crusoe's regeneration: it embodies the didactic impulse traditionally stimulated by conversion, and in its autodidactic aspect strengthens and extends the impact of conversion on Crusoe himself. In short it bears out, at least as dramatically as his celebrated triumphs in pottery and bakery, the impression created by the events leading up to his conversion: that he is a strong vessel whom the Lord "intendeth for strong encounters, and rare employments."

[56] *The Eighteenth Century Background* (N.Y., 1953), p. 17.

Moll Flanders

Spiritual autobiography pursued thematic coherence amid or despite narrative incoherence: incoherence, that is, measured by the more rigorous standards of plotting which the novel was to evolve. So long as the protagonist's inward vicissitudes obeyed the traditional pattern, either of growth or decay, and so long as individual episodes contributed to this pattern with some consistency, an autobiography might be regarded as structurally sound. Within such a convention, whose rationale lay in religious psychology rather than aesthetics, a logic of spiritual change within the character took precedence over a logic of outward action; within such a convention, discrete, apparently random episodes might be held to possess a unity both sufficient and meaningful. This convention, it seems to me, illuminates some basic features of the action and characterization of *Moll Flanders*.[1] The chronological sequence of events is halting and abrupt, and their

[1] Other important features of the book are of course traceable to different conventions, such as those of criminal biography: see Ernest Bernbaum, *The Mary Carleton Narratives 1663–1673* (Cambridge, Mass., 1914), *passim*, and Spiro Peterson, foreword to *The Counterfeit Lady Unveiled* (Garden City, 1961), pp. 4–7. Cf. also Paul Dottin, *Daniel De Foe et ses Romans*, 3 vols. (Paris, 1924), III, 645f.; and John Robert Moore, *Daniel Defoe Citizen of the Modern World* (Chicago, 1958), pp. 242f.

causal connection is arbitrary at best. Between one incident and the next there tends to be some such perfunctory transition as "At length a new scene opened" or "now a new scene of misfortunes attended me" (1, 132, 135). And yet the fact that Moll's story unravels in a series of rather tenuously connected episodes does not rule out an underlying continuity of the kind just described, nor does the abruptness of the outward narrative preclude a gradual, fairly systematic development of the heroine's spiritual condition.

Crusoe's career begins with his running away from home: Defoe supplies no very complex motivation for his act, but anticipates it by establishing his unruliness and obstinacy. Perhaps no single deed so decisively launches the action in *Moll Flanders,* yet the seduction by the elder brother is in some respects comparable. Although Moll's first real act of will, there is little complexity in its motivation: Defoe marshals no more personality traits here than in the opening pages of *Robinson Crusoe.* What he does instead is to emphasize the predominance of a single characteristic— namely, Moll's vanity. Between the ages of eight and fourteen, she develops as strong an obsession about being a gentlewoman as Crusoe's about going to sea. In themselves, both desires may be innocent enough, but each represents a "station in life" which is altogether unnatural and inappropriate under the circumstances. When Moll first speaks of becoming a gentlewoman, she little understands the meaning of the word, but even her naïveté is made slightly ominous.[2] Moreover, from the time she is ten she

[2] Compare the following dialogue between Moll and her old nurse (1, 8): "naming a woman that mended lace and washed the ladies' laced heads; 'she,' says I, 'is a gentlewoman,

begins hearing herself spoken of as pretty, and she confesses that this made her "not a little proud" (1, 9). When at fourteen she enters the family of the Colchester merchant, these combined strains of vanity contribute at least as much as the wiles of the elder brother to her undoing.

That Moll's ambition to become a gentlewoman is not merely an amusing, innocuous irony can be shown in various ways. For one thing, although Defoe was a pioneering advocate of female education, he never speaks of it as a means of social betterment; on the contrary, he always stresses the importance of educating youths not only according to their natural capacities, but according to their expectations.[3] In *Moll Flanders*, the contrast between Moll and the sisters in the family makes clear that her natural capacities are great, but it makes equally clear the discrepancy between her genteel attainments and her prospects in the world.[4] A recurrent theme of contemporary sermons

---

and they call her madam.'

" 'Poor child,' says my good old nurse, 'you may soon be such a gentlewoman as that, for she is a person of ill fame, and has had two bastards.'

"I did not understand anything of that; but I answered, 'I am sure they call her madam, and she does not go to service nor do house-work'; and therefore I insisted that she was a gentlewoman, and I would be such a gentlewoman as that."

[3] Cf. *Serious Reflections*, pp. 63–66. In the section of *An Essay upon Projects* called "An Academy for Women," his proposals are egalitarian only in a special, limited sense: namely, in maintaining that the capacity and the need for education are as great in women as in men. Raising poor orphans to the plane of gentlewomen is not his object.

[4] Compare the sister's speech on p. 15: "Betty wants but one thing, but she had as good want everything, for the market is against our sex just now; and if a young woman has beauty, birth, breeding, wit, sense, manners, modesty, and all to an

and educational tracts was that any such discrepancy is dangerous; Bishop Fleetwood is typical in arguing that "A Parent is to take good heed that he never educate his Children above the Provision he designs to make for them; . . . it being much more easy to bear with a mean Condition constantly, than to fall into it from a plentiful and good one; which is the Case of People better educated than provided for: The soft and tender Usage of People, whilst young, and capable of undergoing Labour and more Hardship, is truly a Diskindness to them, without an answerable Provision for them afterwards; for whenever they are left to shift for themselves, they are no better than expos'd naked, as it were, and defenceless, unable to procure themselves a Livelihood, and in much worse Condition than their Inferiours." The fate of women brought up in such a way, Fleetwood continues, is that they "fall to[o] often into the Hands of wicked Tempters, through want of Ability to employ themselves in honest Courses, and an utter Incapacity of maintaining their Condition; their Poverty makes them unfit for their *Equals*, and their soft Education . . . [makes] their *Inferiours* afraid to match with them." [5] To be sure, Moll does not experience the precise ill effects

---

extreme, yet if she has not money, she's nobody, and had as good want them all." Cf. also *Little Review*, July 4, 1705, p. 33.

[5] *The Relative Duties of Parents and Children, Husbands and Wives, Masters and Servants; Consider'd in Sixteen Practical Discourses* . . . , 3rd edition (1722), pp. 100–01, 102; cf. Robert Moss, *The Providential Division of Men into Rich and Poor, and the respective Duties thence arising* . . . (1708), p. 22. Moss's is a charity-school anniversary sermon; such occasions frequently called for remarks resembling Fleetwood's.

that Fleetwood predicts, yet the point is made that her education not only exceeds her provision but renders her vulnerable to temptation. Thus the very word "gentlewoman" at first means no more than self-support, and later signifies genteel appearance and attainments; yet it becomes increasingly associated with money, so that the longer Moll's education in gentility continues, the more susceptible she is to gold as well as "fine words" (1, 20).

At all events, Defoe takes care to indicate that it is vanity rather than love or lust which animates her at the beginning. Although in the course of time she does become passionately attached to the elder brother, this does not seem to be a factor in her initial seduction. When the elder brother's declarations of love "fire her blood," it is her vanity which is enflamed; [6] and when the courtship is well under way, she makes the significant distinction that "This gentleman had now fired *his* inclination as much as he had *my* vanity." [7] Throughout the book Defoe is careful to distinguish between what is done from "gust" or "inclination" and what is done from other motives. Here, instead of positively denying that Moll shares the brother's "inclination," he remains silent about this possibility, and makes Moll dwell exclusively on the element of vanity. The reason, I think, is not that he intends to lessen her

[6] Thus Moll reports that "my head ran upon strange things, and I may truly say I was not myself, to have such a gentleman talk to me of being in love with me, and of my being such a charming creature, as he told me I was. These things I knew not how to bear; my vanity was elevated to the last degree" (1, 17).

[7] 1, 19; italics mine. Even at the climactic moment (1, 24), it is the sight of the purse and the fire of the proposal that cause Moll's color to come and go, not any passion on her part.

guilt by clearing her of any anticipatory relish for the deed itself, but on the contrary that he wants to stress her own vanity as the force that really prevails over her virtue.[8] By furnishing the elder brother with subtlety and cash, and by placing Moll in what amounts to the situation of a chambermaid[9]—an extremely vulnerable one at the time, as Pamela Andrews was to discover—Defoe does take into account the external forces that contribute to her seduction; but such forces by no means lessen her own responsibility for the deed. They scarcely even complicate her choice, but instead give impetus to that vanity which alone determines her behavior.

It has seemed worth dwelling on this initial action for several reasons. In the first place, it must be acknowledged that Defoe takes pains with the narrative itself, but his attitude towards it resembles that of a recent fictional narrator who declares, "I have always been deeply interested in the administrative side of love. . . . What Lady Chatterley and her gamekeeper did in the woods is, to me, of only passing interest, compared with how they got there." [10] Insofar as Defoe is concerned with the outward story of the seduction, it is "the administrative side" that absorbs his attention, as the elder brother's final elaborate ruse well illustrates. The economic implications of the deed

[8] Moll states emphatically that "that which I was too vain of was my ruin, or rather my vanity was the cause of it" (I, 14); and she calls herself "a fair memento to all young women whose vanity prevails over their virtue" (I, 21).

[9] On this point, see Novak, *Economics and the Fiction of Daniel Defoe*, pp. 84–85.

[10] Malcolm Muggeridge, *Affairs of the Heart*, quoted in *New York Times* review by Nigel Dennis, March 5, 1961, VIII, 5.

fall into this category, it seems to me. While it is true that they figure more prominently than any erotic aspects of the affair, they remain one item in "the administrative side," rather than themselves constituting the controlling factor, or the ultimate significance of what takes place.[11]

Indeed, a second reason for looking closely at these early scenes is that they show, in a way that seems characteristic of Defoe, economic considerations being subsumed under moral ones; gold takes its place, along with flattery but no more crucially, as one of the stimuli to Moll's vanity. And although various forces act on Moll from without, they do not make for a corresponding complexity of "personal characteristics": the complexity remains external, while she herself is dominated by the single characteristic of vanity. Her vanity may itself take various outward forms, but nevertheless provides a radically simple basis for Moll's thoughts and actions at this point in the book.

This, then, is a final reason for attending to the preliminaries of Moll's seduction, for despite the complication of the external narrative, there is nothing very intricate about Moll's own character. Without wishing to generalize from this single episode, one might anticipate her subsequent treatment by saying it consists of complex outward manifestations of inward states that are in fact rather simple. To return to the initial argument, the book's real coherence seems to lie in the gradual unfolding of these inward states, not

[11] For a reading of *Moll Flanders* which places greater emphasis on its economic aspects, see Denis Donoghue, "The Values of *Moll Flanders*," *Sewanee Review*, LXXI (1963), pp. 287–303.

in the overt action by which they are revealed. If we take Moll's vanity as a point of departure, analogous to Crusoe's rebelliousness, we find a certain consistency in the vicissitudes that follow, however disconnected they may be outwardly.

There are several points of comparison, in fact, between Moll's and Crusoe's spiritual careers. In the first place, each has the repeated option of altering his course after the original misdeed. In Crusoe's case, unmediated acts of Providence function as calls to conversion which go unheeded. Moll remains within society, and is less subject to direct, elemental threats and deliverances, but in the course of her dealings with other people she experiences recurrent promptings to repentance. Instead of resisting or neglecting them, as does Crusoe, she entertains them momentarily, or partially, or insincerely, so that her career is marked by a series of false starts. Secondly, lacking religious conviction to direct or sanction her behavior, Moll acts (to use a phrase from *Robinson Crusoe*) "like a mere brute from the principles of Nature, and by the dictates of common sense only, and indeed hardly that" (p. 97). As in *Robinson Crusoe*, Defoe indicates that practical reason is a weak and faltering guide; not only is Moll's judgment overcome on crucial occasions by external pressures or inducements, but it is rendered ineffectual by the gradual enslavement of her will. Finally, there is an essential likeness in the kind of spiritual development Crusoe and Moll undergo: indeed, the two features just noted can be seen as corollaries of this more basic pattern. Gradual hardening characterizes Crusoe's career prior to conversion, although this is made fully explicit only when he comes to repent. Moll's actions lack the traditional symbolic overtones that Crusoe's have; to compensate for this, and to make clear that she is undergoing the classic process of hardening, the significance of many episodes is spelled out as they occur.

As for the first of these three features, Moll's abortive repentances begin fairly soon after the seduction. When the younger brother proposes marriage, she exclaims that "I was now in a dreadful condition indeed, and now I repented heartily my easiness with the eldest brother; not from any reflection of conscience, for I was a stranger to those things, but I could not think of being a whore to one brother and a wife to the other" (1, 27). Here "repentance" is largely a matter of worldly prudence, and is very remote from its true nature, as defined in Defoe's other works and later in this one. But that Moll is not speaking altogether casually is indicated by the parenthesis, "not from any reflection of conscience, for I was a stranger to those things." Here and in similar passages, Defoe clearly means to stress the ironic contrast between Moll's passing qualms and real repentance.[12]

Sometimes Moll does not speak of repenting, but describes herself as seriously considering or reflecting. Again there is often a more or less explicit contrast with the opening stage of genuine repentance, discussed earlier. On these occasions, however, the irony

[12] The conclusion of the passage introduces a note of squeamishness which also deserves comment. As the story proceeds, Moll repeatedly draws lines at certain kinds of wrongdoing out of a bizarre compunction, less moral than aesthetic or sentimental, and balks at actions scarcely more wicked than those which have become habitual to her. Besides being a piece of femininity that contributes to the book's "formal realism," this trait should probably be regarded as a specimen of Moll's tendency to swallow camels and strain at gnats, about which more will be said.

of the contrast tends to be less pronounced than when Moll actually talks of repentance. Thus when the younger brother persists in his open courtship, and Moll's dilemma requires the elder brother's advice, she says "Upon serious consideration, for indeed now I began to consider things very seriously, and never till now, I resolved to tell him of it" (1, 28). When she is living in the Mint, and finds she is "not wicked enough for such fellows" as the debauched debtors who take refuge there, she asserts that "I began to consider here very seriously what I had to do; how things stood with me, and what course I ought to take" (1, 64). When her liaison with the man at Bath is over, she reports that "I cast about innumerable ways for my future state of life, and began to consider very seriously what I should do" (1, 130). When she has parted with her Lancashire lover and returns to lodgings in London, she says that "here being perfectly alone, I had leisure to sit down and reflect seriously upon the last seven months' ramble I had made" (1, 165). Soon after the delivery of her son by this "marriage," she receives a letter from her London clerk, in which he announces his divorce, the suicide of his ex-wife, and his hope of seeing Moll again: her reaction is that "I was exceedingly surprised at the news, and began now seriously to reflect on my circumstances" (1, 178).

These are a few of the reflections and considerations that punctuate Moll's career before she commits her first theft. Each bout comes at a crucial point in her affairs, but dissipates itself in worldly scheming. I do not wish to imply that Defoe invariably associates the terms "serious consideration" and "serious reflection" with incipient repentance, so that any other use of them on Moll's part involves irony. But it does appear significant that each time she is afforded an opportunity to review and alter her course of action, her attention quickly shifts from self-scrutiny to outward reconnoitering. In any case, subsequent passages lend weight to the supposition that her terminology in the above instances is not entirely casual or unconscious. When she later describes the character of the gentleman she meets at Bartholomew Fair, she recognizes that his capacity for making "just reflections" on his behavior falls considerably short of genuine, durable repentance (II, 48). And when she comes to describe her own "lethargy of soul" in Newgate, she begins by putting it negatively: she has no sense of her condition despite the fact that, as she admits, "I had a weight of guilt upon me, enough to sink any creature with the least power of reflection left" (II, 94). In other words, her lowest spiritual ebb is marked by the loss (or total abeyance) of that "power of reflection" which she had long stifled, or at best diverted to external, worldly matters from its proper object: the state of her soul.

Taken by themselves, Moll's spells of serious reflection may seem inconclusive. Running parallel to them, however, is the series of insincere or incomplete repentances mentioned earlier. One instance has already been cited. A more striking one, which could be called a case of sentimental repentance, occurs at the time of her marriage to the London clerk. When she accepts the clerk's proposal, he is "so overcome with the satisfaction of it" that "tears stand in his eyes," upon which Moll declares that "I turned from him, for it filled my eyes with tears too, and asked him leave to retire a little to my chamber. If I had a grain of true repentance for an abominable life of twenty-four years past, it was then" (I, 190). And after she is married, she reports that "I sat many an hour by myself, and wept over the remembrance of past follies, and the dreadful extravagances of a wicked life, and sometimes I flattered myself that I had sincerely repented" (I, 197). Weeping may, as we have seen, be a symptom of genuine "conviction," but here it merely provides emotional release. Moll's tearful sentimentality might, like her squeamishness, be no more than a feminine trait included for the sake of realism, and accounts of her outward personality should certainly mention her frequent weeping along with her unscrupulous hardness. But such sentimentality actually provides a further contrast with the nature of true repentance. This is made particularly clear when Moll steals the bundle of plate from the burning house. She confesses that "the inhumanity of this action moved me very much, and made me relent exceedingly, and tears stood in my eyes upon that subject; but with all my sense of its being cruel and inhuman, I could never find in my heart to make any restitution. The reflection wore off, and I quickly forgot the circumstances that attended it" (II, 14). Here most of the ingredients of repentance already singled out are strikingly combined: what with tears and revulsion, relenting and reflecting, Moll would seem to be in a fair way to repent, yet her remaining moral awareness spends itself in sentimental indulgence, and the upshot is only further hardening.[13]

The full significance of this series of abortive re-

[13] It is also at this point that the pretense of necessity gives way to frank avarice; indeed her refusal to make restitution marks not only the remoteness of this outburst from true repentance, but also the obsessive wish to gain "a little more, and a little more" (II, 15).

pentances will become clear when the final, effectual one is examined. One further passage may be noted, however, since it illustrates Defoe's care in distinguishing real repentance from false or partial versions. When Moll is first committed to Newgate, she makes the following statement: "Then I repented heartily of all my life past, but that repentance yielded me no satisfaction, no peace, no, not in the least, because, as I said to myself, it was repenting after the power of further sinning was taken away. I seemed not to mourn that I had committed such crimes, and for the fact, as it was an offense against God and my neighbour, but that I was to be punished for it. I was a penitent, as I thought, not that I had sinned, but that I was to suffer, and this took away all the comfort of my repentance in my own thoughts" (II, 89–90). The implied distinction is a sophisticated but important one, as contemporary discussions of fear as a basis for repentance (cited above, page 109, note 41) strongly indicate. Within a very few pages Moll is to undergo a repentance that is clearly meant to be valid, but here, to offset any suspicion that she is a mere gallows-penitent, Defoe gives us a brief specimen of this kind of pseudo-repentance, and makes the point that it *is* hollow and ineffectual. Prompted by the imminence of punishment, rather than by actual abhorrence of sin, and seeking neither forgiveness nor comfort from God, such "repentance" can issue only in despair: thus Moll is oppressed by thoughts of "nothing night or day, but of gibbets and halters, evil spirits and devils" (II, 93). These partial or false repentances contribute to the book in several ways. Through their very recurrence, they provide one thematic link between outwardly diverse episodes; through their implicit contrast with real repentance, they help to characterize Moll's spiritual state as they occur; finally, they are among the factors that heighten the significance of the genuine repentance which finally takes place.

I have described a second feature of Moll's vicissitudes, between her initial misstep and her conversion, as an adherence to that weak and faltering guide, her own reason. Much has been written about Defoe's faith in human reason, but the evidence in *Moll Flanders*, as in *Robinson Crusoe*, points to an attitude by no means sanguine. Moll's reasoning is mentioned almost as frequently as her reflecting and considering, but it is no more reliable a guide. Indeed, on two crucial occasions she speaks of being "reasoned out of her reason." This is the phrase she uses first to describe the effect of the elder brother's arguments in favor of her marrying the younger brother (I, 54), and she uses it again to characterize the governess's sophistic invalidation of her Lancashire marriage (I, 180). Perhaps the most notable instance in Defoe's fiction of the speciousness of "reason" when pitted against morality occurs in *Roxana*, in the long debate with the Dutch merchant over female independence (I, 167f.), but these two scenes in *Moll Flanders* make the same point. With "reason" (such as it is) as her guide, rather than religious conviction, Moll is vulnerable to the plausible arguments of wicked counselors.

If this were all, however, we might be justified in regarding "reason" as merely one of the external forces which Moll alleges in extenuation of her misdeeds. But Defoe goes further, to lay responsibility squarely with Moll herself. He displays the fundamental inadequacy of reason to cope not only with the devil's advocates, but also with Moll's own conflicting inclinations. In other words, even when reason is not threatened by sophistry from without, it is liable to be undermined from within by emotions too strong for it. Thus we find Moll admitting, when she determines to marry the "gentleman tradesman," that "I was hurried on (by my fancy to a gentleman) to ruin myself in the grossest manner that ever woman did" (1, 58). We may recall Crusoe confessing in the same vein that in undertaking the slaving voyage "I was hurried on, and obeyed blindly the dictates of my fancy rather than my reason" (p. 43). Defoe appears to have believed that no principle, however rationally discovered or adhered to, is proof against the power of "fancy" or irrational impulse unless it is buttressed by religious conviction.[14] Earlier discussion of Robinson Crusoe's and Robert Drury's motives for going to sea has shown how much force Defoe attaches to "inclination" as a spring of action, and how deeply skeptical he is of it. He not only fails to share the optimistic faith, becom-

---

[14] The behavior of Moll's Bath lover affords a good illustration of this. He spends a night in bed with her, but she reports that he "rose up and dressed him in the morning, and left me as innocent for him as the day I was born"; nor, as she is careful to observe, "did he act thus on a principle of religion at all, but of mere affection" (1, 117). "I own it was a noble principle," she further remarks, and he manages to maintain it for some time. But one night, "owing to our having yielded too far to our mutual inclinations," as Moll explains (1, 121), she "exchanged the place of friend for that unmusical, harsh-sounding title of whore" (1, 118). Thus a "principle" of behavior, unfortified by religious conviction, ultimately gives way before powerful inclination. Cf. also Defoe's remark in *Applebee's Journal* for March 18, 1721, that "It is Religion alone, which is the Bond of Virtue in the World; the Awe of a Divine Power, and a Sense of the Majesty and Vengeance of Heaven, being alone able to restrain the Vices and Lusts of Men" (Lee, *Life and Recently Discovered Writings*, II, 353).

ing current in his day, that human "gust" or impulse is naturally towards the good, but he doubts that inclination, even when it is clearly malignant, can be checked by mere reason. This belief might be shown by tracing the workings of reason and inclination in greater detail, but it also emerges from the portrait of Moll's gradual hardening.

I have suggested that between her seduction and her conversion, a process of hardening makes up the basic pattern of her spiritual development. That she undergoes some kind of hardening is clear from her own repeated admissions, so that even critics who deny the presence of any meaningful structure in the book recognize this as a prominent feature of Moll's psychological make-up. But the traditional significance of this hardening process and its specific function in the book remain to be investigated. Earlier chapters have alluded to it briefly, pointing out that in both spiritual autobiography and its fictional derivants, some degree of hardening inevitably attends any prolonged delay in conversion, and that the stages of such hardening often supply the principle for selecting and organizing the events narrated prior to conversion.

The first thing to emphasize about hardness of heart is that it is in fact a spiritual state, not merely a psychological one. To be sure, its manifestations are of a kind nowadays approached psychologically. But so long as men continued to believe in the reality and importance of the soul, psychology remained largely a method of analyzing and describing the state of a soul through its outward workings. It is not that the psychological and the spiritual were opposed: the description and analysis might have the precision we associate with science, but their ultimate object was spiritual.

The evidence for these contentions has already been given. They are reintroduced here as a reminder that hardness of heart is essentially a spiritual phenomenon, and that even the most painstaking narrations of it may have spiritual assessment rather than psychological realism as their purpose.

A second and more obvious point about spiritual hardening is precisely that it is a process. Like regeneration, the term "hardness of heart" can represent a fully realized state, but it more commonly stands for an ongoing, cumulative development.[15] It is not reached instantaneously, through a single misdeed, any more than is regeneration achieved through the bare experience of conversion: each requires time and persistence.[16] In any case, a traditional conception of hardness of heart as something essentially spiritual, not merely psychological, and as an unfolding process, not an absolute state, stands in the background of Defoe's treatment of the theme in *Moll Flanders*.

[15] The notion of hardness of heart as a gradual process gave rise to fairly elaborate attempts at schematization. But owing perhaps to the wide variation between observed cases, or perhaps simply to the lack of authoritative Biblical or patristic models, the steps in hardening were never entirely standardized. What may be the most ambitious "brief of the degrees of hardness" during the period is the section of Joseph Caryl's commentary on Job 9:4, in which nine separate steps are distinguished: see his *Exposition . . . of Job*, 1, 763–64. Cf. also Samuel Wright, *A Treatise on the Deceitfulness of Sin; And its leading Men to Hardness of Heart: With the Means Appointed to prevent both its Hardning and Deceiving*, 5th edition (1735; 1st edition, 1726), pp. 62–71.

[16] On the role of custom or habit in hardening the heart, see Robert Bolton, *Some Generall Directions for a Comfortable Walking with God*, 5th edition (1638), p. 233; William Bates, "How to Bear Afflictions," *Cripplegate Exercises*, 11, 590; Taylor, *Unum Necessarium*, in *Works*, vii, 151; Tillotson, "Of the Difficulty of reforming Vicious Habits," in *Works*, ii, 195.

It is true that Moll's hardening is portrayed in greatest detail during her actual criminal career, and some critics have seen it as beginning only with her first theft. Nevertheless it can be maintained that she undergoes gradual hardening from the point of her seduction, so that the process gives a continuity to her behavior throughout the larger part of the book.[17] She explicitly alludes to it on more than one occasion, but her very qualms and revulsions afford evidence that this is actually her situation. It may seem paradoxical to argue that her recurrent squeamishness is a symptom of hardening, but I think this is the case. If so, it helps to solve a problem in her characterization that has disturbed various critics. This problem, and one possible solution to it, are stated as follows in James Sutherland's stimulating introduction to a recent edition of the book: "As Moll grows old in crime, Defoe is concerned to show us how her moral arteries harden, and it may now be objected, more plausibly than ever, that such a woman would no longer be capable of the tenderness and the moral scruples that Moll continues from time to time to show. But to say that is to have too rigid a conception of human character. . . . Moll has the inconsistency that comes from being alive; she lives for the moment, and she changes with circumstances."[18]

The inconsistency may be only apparent, however.

[17] Even while she remains in Colchester, her initial vanity grows into something more baneful, as her remarks on the death of the younger brother indicate (1, 56). Bearing in mind the care taken to establish vanity rather than lust as the basis of her initial compliance, one sees that her guilt is compounded, not reduced, when the younger brother makes her an honest woman. The trouble is not that she fails to love him, but that her attachment to the elder brother, which she retains rather than repents, assumes new proportions.

[18] (Boston, 1959), p. xv.

If we take into account the kind of behavior traditionally associated with hardening, Moll's periodic
scruples are not really self-contradictory. They tend
to follow the pattern described in a typical sermon "Of
the Danger, Nature, and Malignity of a Hard-Heart":
". . . it is with Conscience, as with a Dog that keeps a
Country-House, tho' he opens and runs fiercely at a
Stranger, yet he lies still and is silent when any of the
Family comes in; and the frequent Conversation at the
House, will in some time so perfectly reconcile him to
the Stranger, that he will not bite, nor so much as move
his Tongue against him. We may easily observe in
Men great Reluctance to some new Sins, who indulge
themselves at the same time in others never a whit less
criminal; and a little Time and familiar Practice will
take off their Prejudice against those Vices, at which
for the present they are very clamorous." [19] Naturally
what William Hopkins has in mind is most pronounced at the very outset of a sinful career, and this
part of his argument is duplicated by various writers
on habitual sin.[20] But what is particularly relevant to
the issue raised by Mr. Sutherland is the observation
that men have "great Reluctance to some new Sins,
who indulge themselves at the same time in others

[19] *Seventeen Sermons of the Reverend and Learned Dr.
William Hopkins* (1708), p. 294; cf. pp. 299–300.

[20] Indeed, the idea traces back to Augustine, who had asserted that "At first we are ashamed of sin; but custom makes
us bold and confident, apt to proclaim, not to conceal our
shame. For though at first it seemed great, yet every day of
use makes it less, and at last all is well, it is a very nothing"
(paraphrased by Jeremy Taylor, *Unum Necessarium*, in
Works, VII, 170). Cf. Tillotson's simile comparing sinners with travellers, in his sermon "Of the Deceitfulness and
Danger of Sin," *Works*, I, 207.

never a whit less criminal"; for it is this tendency that largely accounts for Moll's scruples, and resolves their apparent inconsistency. I have spoken of the way her sentimental and partial repentances reveal, by ironic contrast with real repentance, her actual impenitence, and the way her fleeting "reflections" and "considerations" indicate, through a similar contrast with genuine self-scrutiny, her actual spiritual torpor. Her scruples should probably be regarded in the same light: they do not belie her hardening, but illustrate its very progress; they do not contradict but confirm it.

Turning to specific instances, we find that Moll is subject to various scruples after parting from her Lancashire husband, and before marrying the London clerk. She proves pregnant, which is "a perplexing thing" on several accounts. She declares at one point that "indeed I would have been glad to miscarry, but I could never entertain so much as a thought of taking anything to make me miscarry; I abhorred, I say, so much as the thought of it" (1, 167; cf. 1, 175). The child is born, but must be gotten out of the way if Moll is to marry the London clerk. As mentioned earlier, she has scruples even about the legality of contracting a new marriage, but her governess manages to reason her out of her reason. The old lady, whom Moll has learned to call mother, is equally resourceful and accommodating in the matter of disposing of the child. She proposes that Moll "must do even as other conscientious mothers have done" before her, and give it to one of the people who are paid "to take the child off the parent's hands, and to take care of it as long as it lives" (1, 182), although as Moll recognizes, the practice amounts to "a contrived method for murder; that is to say, killing [one's] children with safety" (1, 180).[21] But Moll strenuously dissociates herself from the whores, the "conscientious mothers" who avail themselves of all the governess's facilities: "let me be what I would," she affirms, "I was not come up to that pitch of hardness, common to the profession" (1, 183). She lays particular stress on the bonds of nature and affection which link her to the child, contrasting herself with the governess, who, "as she was hardened in these things beyond all possibility of being touched with the religious part, and the scruples about the murder, so she was equally impenetrable in that part which related to affection" (1, 181).

What are we to make of Moll's protestations throughout this scene? On the assumption that they are genuine, is it Defoe's intention that we admire and sympathize with her? If so, does the whole bizarre setting make her nevertheless an object of unintended irony? Or does Defoe mean us to condemn Moll? Has he made her sympathetic in spite of himself? A case could be made for each possibility, but I believe the third is the correct one. We are to take Moll at her word. She puts things comparatively: she is not as hardened as the other inmates at the Sign of the Cradle, or its proprietor. She has become reconciled to a great deal, but she still has strong qualms about abortion and infanticide, and faint residual scruples about bigamy. In Hopkins's terms, she shows "great Reluctance to some new Sins," even though her old ones do not weigh heavily upon her. She is not altogether hardened, but hardening, and because this is a gradual

[21] On this practice, see Defoe's proposal for erecting a foundling hospital in *Augusta Triumphans* (1728).

process, not a simple state of being, she can accept some things and balk at others without real self-contradiction. What is required for consistency's sake is merely that she accept more and more, and balk at less and less.

Nor do I think the essentially critical view of Moll at this stage of her career is weakened, much less negated, by anything unintentionally sympathetic in the portrait. I have spoken of Moll's recurrent tearfulness as a characteristic of her shallow and abortive pseudo-repentances, and there is little reason to suppose that her sentimentality on this occasion is any more redeeming. Moreover, it is significant that she appeals to nature and affection in her abhorrence of doing away with the child. Here, as in her discussion of the Bath lover's "noble principle," she sharply distinguishes between religion and affection as sanctions of action. By this time there should be little doubt that Defoe attaches a very equivocal value to "affection," and regards it at best as a fitful and precarious guide.[22] When he speaks of "affection," he invests it with little intrinsic or independent merit as a moral sentiment, and displays little faith in benevolence and fellow-feeling: it may place scruples in the way of

[22] For Defoe's evaluation of "affection," compare n. 14 above, and the following passage from *Street-Robberies, Consider'd* [1728], p. 10: "I was no sooner brought into this World to breath freer Air, but my Mother thought me as great a Burthen to her as she did the Day before I was Born, therefore thought of many Stratagems to get rid of me, at least to procure something for my Support; for she own'd she had some small Affection for me. She got a Hand-Basket, into which, pretty late, she put my Worship, and ty'd me Decently to a Knocker of a Door in *Cornhill*, (for I was a Citizen born) and then stood aloof to see the Event."

vice, but, if unsupported by religious conviction, it cannot withstand strong temptation or contrary inclination.

The scruples to which Mr. Sutherland actually refers, however, are those that continue to beset Moll after she has begun her career of theft. These may admit of the same explanation: rather than belying her hardening, they are symptomatic of it. All her palpitations over the first theft might seem to indicate that her hardening really begins only at this point. Her initial essay in shoplifting undeniably marks another fresh start in the narrative, but there does not seem to be any comparable break in her spiritual development. We may recall that she says of her years with the banker's clerk, "sometimes I flattered myself that I had sincerely repented." Partial repentance may cause a change in outward behavior, and, given favorable circumstances, such changes may be lasting. But such "repentance" does not alter, or even interrupt, one's inward decline. As we observed in connection with Crusoe's career, the failure to repent efficaciously of old sins is spiritually equivalent to the commission of new ones. In these terms, then, Moll's five virtuous years do not preclude the continuity of her spiritual decay.

In other words, her career in crime is not so much a case of innocence giving way to guilt, as of existing guilt taking on new degrees and dimensions. It is true that she is moved to steal out of necessity. Her initial theft is extenuated, if not fully condoned, by the fact that there are "temptations which it is not in the power of human nature to resist." [23] But she notes in the same

[23] I, 197; cf. Maximillian Novak's interesting article on "The Problem of Necessity in Defoe's Fiction," *PQ*, XL (1961),

sentence that "as covetousness is the root of all evil, so poverty is the worst of all snares"; what is so sinister about the first theft is that poverty opens a breach for covetousness. As she had observed of an earlier lapse, with the Bath lover, "the way being thus cleared, and the bars of virtue and conscience thus removed, we had the less to struggle with" (1, 118). Thus necessity may justify the initial misdeed, but if repentance does not follow, the lapse becomes a settled course of action, which in turn is culpable whatever the original provocation.[24] In taking this attitude towards Moll's

pp. 513–24. Mr. Novak is most informative on secular theories of natural law in the seventeenth century; on one point, however, his remarks seem to me misleading. Speaking of Defoe's "failure to distinguish between poverty and necessity," Mr. Novak says that "If he has little authority from the philosophers for this radical departure, he has even less from the religious treatises of his fellow Dissenters," and he goes on to quote Matthew Henry and Richard Baxter to the effect that necessity is not a sufficient justification for theft. But for the equation between poverty and necessity, see Timothy Cruso, *Discourses Upon the Rich Man and Lazarus* (1697), p. 24; for the same equation, and the view that necessity may justify theft, see Francis Osborne's essay on Proverbs 30:8 in his *Works*, 8th edition (1682), pp. 514, 518–19 and *passim*. For further evidence that Defoe's equation of poverty and necessity marks no "radical departure," compare the following statement by Samuel Butler: "Poverty and want are greater Temptations than Riches; when our Savior had fasted 40 days, and as many Nights, the Devil thought it the fittest time to attack him: and St. Peter denyd and forswore Christ when he saw him in Affliction. For wealth and Luxury can but Tempt: Necessity compel's." ("Religion," in *Characters and Passages from Note-Books*, edited by A. R. Waller [Cambridge, 1908], p. 298.) A very ample and intelligent discussion of these questions, which Defoe is likely to have read, occurs in Part IV of Jeremy Collier's *Essays upon several Moral Subjects* (1709); "Of Theft" occupies pp. 264–361, and these topics are considered especially at pp. 326–31.

[24] It should be noted that it is the *anticipation* of poverty,

crimes, Defoe is neither rigid nor lax, but stands in a humane tradition. Admitting a legitimate plea in defense of an isolated lapse, he nevertheless deplores the tendency of one sin to make way for others, and treats the habitual sin with due severity. His demonstration of the way single misdeeds become habitual sins, however, is more interesting than his judgment of the one or the other.

This process begins with the scene following the theft. At first Moll is under "dreadful impressions of fear, and in such terrors of mind, though I was perfectly safe, that I cannot express the manner of it" (1, 201). She speculates that she may have robbed some poor widow like herself, and this thought torments her for several days.[25] Yet her own distresses silence these reflections, and she reports that "the prospect of my own starving . . . hardened my heart by degrees" (1, 202). She is still able to pray for deliverance, although she confesses that "my prayers had no hope in them . . . it was all fear without and dark within; and I reflected on my past life as not repented of, that Heaven was now beginning to punish me, and would make me as miserable as I had been wicked" (*ibid.*). Her final comment is that "Had I gone on here I had perhaps been a true penitent," but as on previous occasions, her "reflections" and convictions subside. At this point, then, her criminal career is at a stage frequently described by divines by the simile of a spring, easily dammed at first but quickly becom-

---

rather than the *fact* of it, that afflicts Moll: thus she says "I saw nothing before me but the utmost distress; and this represented itself so lively to my thoughts, that it seemed as if it had come, before it was really very near" (1, 199).

[25] For partial analogues to this scene, see *Colonel Jacque*, 1, 72–73, 96–100; *Street-Robberies, Consider'd*, p. 20f.

ing a flood if allowed to proceed. A notable statement
from Jeremy Taylor, enforcing the argument that sins
eventually "destroy the soul by their abode, who at
their first entry might have been killed with the pressure of a little finger," has already been quoted.[26] This
principle finds expression in autobiographical narrative
in *An Alarme for Sinners* (1679). Robert Foulkes,
who could speak with some authority, observes that
"the heights of wickedness appear so monstrous at a
distance to one that is but newly entering upon it, that
he flatters himself he shall never come thither; but after
long continuance in it, and suppressing many Convictions, violating our Vows and Resolutions, after many
Evasions to shift off the imputation, apologies to excuse or lessen it, . . . a man becomes strangely altered" (pp. 9–10). By failing to repent of this sin at its
"first entry," Moll eases the way for its further onsets.
Moreover, once she has quelled her first "dreadful
impressions," she readily finds the kind of evasions and
apologies that Foulkes speaks of. Thus her second
"adventure," when she takes the child's necklace,
causes her "no great concern": she rationalizes that "as
I did the child no harm, I only thought I had given the
parents a just reproof for their negligence, in leaving
the poor lamb to come home by itself, and it would
teach them to take more care another time" (1, 204).
(The phrase "I only thought" should perhaps be emphasized; Defoe makes clear that this is the way Moll
excused or lessened the crime at the time, not when she
came to write of it.[27])

[26] See above, p. 19. The same image is used by Whichcote,
Select Sermons (Edinburgh, 1742), p. 93; cf. also Austen, *The
Spirituall use of an Orchard*, p. 98.
[27] On this passage, see Watt, *The Rise of the Novel*, p. 124.
Postulating a Puritan "tendency for the individual to be mer-

In the episodes that follow, Defoe skillfully under-
mines Moll's "Evasions to shift off the imputation."
We have seen that he makes Crusoe repeat the substance of his original sin, so that what might have
seemed an isolated lapse is shown to become an in-
grained pattern of action. He achieves the same effect
here by placing Moll in the household of her old
governess. Here she is able to live cheaply, and to farm
out her son by the banker's clerk (which she now does
with no compunction); most important, she gets
"some quilting work for ladies' beds, petticoats, and
the like" (II, 5). The result is that her pretexts for
thieving are removed: "but as poverty brought me in,"
she confesses, "so avarice kept me in, till there was no
going back" (II, 10).[28] Thus covetousness, rather than

---

cifully blind to his own faults"—a tendency scarcely characteristic of the diarists and autobiographers we have examined
—Mr. Watt maintains that Moll Flanders frequently exempli-
fies it, and cites this passage as evidence. But what Defoe gives
us here is the immediate response of Moll the protagonist, not
the retrospective judgment of Moll the narrator. In an autobiography, real or fictional, such phrases as "I only thought"
make a great difference; by means of them, Defoe can differ-
entiate between Moll's initial evasiveness and her point of
view as regenerate narrator. For another view of this scene,
however, see Howard L. Koonce, "Moll's Muddle: Defoe's
Use of Irony in *Moll Flanders*," *ELH*, xxx (1963), pp. 378–
79. Cf. also A. A. Mendilow, "The Time Locus of the Pseudo-
Author," in *Time and the Novel* (1952), pp. 89–93; and
Wayne Booth, *The Rhetoric of Fiction* (Chicago, 1961), pp.
321–22.

[28] The following remarks in the second volume of *The
Compleat English Tradesman* (1727) illuminate the connection between necessity and avarice: "every Station of Life has
its Snares attending it, and every Degree of Business has its
Invitation to do Evil:

1. Necessity tempts the poor Man.
2. Avarice tempts the rich.

It is true, they are both, to the last Degree, criminal in yield-

narrow circumstances, becomes her sole motivation. From the first she had been legally guilty; now the moral blame too is entirely hers.

It is clear from Defoe's other works that he believed in the existence of the devil, and it is worth inquiring briefly whether Moll's allusions to him involve any lessening or transfer of her own responsibility. It seems to me that they do not. At first it was the devil who "laid the snare" and prompted her, "as if he had spoke," to snatch the bundle from the apothecary's shop: yet there is no attempt to represent the actual theft as anything other than a fully voluntary act. But when she reaches the point that avarice "keeps her in," Moll speaks of the devil as follows: "Thus I, that was once in the devil's clutches, was held fast there as with a charm, and had no power to go without the circle, till I was engulfed in labyrinths of trouble too great to get out at all" (II, 10). This might seem to imply that some external power, rather than Moll herself, is responsible. But this is probably not Defoe's intention. Instead, he may be representing her spiritual condition in quite conventional terms, for hardening in sin had long been described as a kind of impotence, and as a kind of slavery to Satan. The origin of these metaphors is Biblical: thus Tillotson points out that "to express to

---

ing to the Temptation; but the latter much more than the former; for he is tempted by that which is in itself a Crime: 'Tis not criminal to be poor; Necessity is no Offence till it makes itself a Snare, and places itself in the *Devil's* Stead: But *Avarice* is a Crime in its Nature; . . . The first is an Accident to the Man, a Circumstance of Life, and comes from without; but Avarice is within the Man; 'tis mingled, as we say, with his Animal Life; it runs in his Blood; it has insinuated itself into his very Species, and he is truly, as the Text says, *drawn aside by his own Lust, and enticed*" (Introduction, pp. 21–22).

us the miserable condition of such persons, [Scripture] representeth them as perfect slaves to their vices, that have sold themselves to do wickedness, and *are led captive by Satan at his pleasure.*" [29] These remarks are typical of seventeenth- and early-eighteenth-century discussions of habitual sin, of which the most powerful and influential may be the fifth chapter of Jeremy Taylor's *Unum Necessarium.* In any case, they provide a helpful gloss to Moll's talk about being held fast in the devil's clutches, and having no power to get out of them. Far from diminishing her own guilt, such statements seem intended to show just how grave her situation has become.[30]

Moreover, the passage just quoted helps to account for the "moral scruples" she continues to feel. Hardened by success, her will is becoming enslaved, but her understanding is not yet darkened. Her case still resembles that expressed by St. Paul's "What I would, that do I not, but what I hate, that do I" (Romans

[29] "Of the Deceitfulness and Danger of Sin," in *Works,* I, 209; he is paraphrasing John 8:44. Elsewhere he observes that "Habit and Custom is a kind of second nature; and so far as any thing is natural, so far it is necessary, and we cannot do otherwise. By passing from one degree of sin to another, Men become fix'd and harden'd in their Wickedness, and do insensibly bring themselves into that state, out of which they are utterly unable to recover themselves" ("The Necessity of Supernatural Grace, in order to a Christian Life," in *Works,* VIII, 504). Cf. also Edward Waple, *Thirty Sermons,* p. 94.

[30] Moll's references to fate are probably to be regarded in the same light; compare, for instance, the statement that "It seemed to me that I was hurried on by an inevitable fate to this day of misery" (II, 89). Defoe holds that the Devil really does exist and that "Fate" does not, but the point is that neither power actually dictates Moll's behavior from without; both serve primarily to objectify compulsions within her, for which she herself is responsible.

7:15), and by the frequently quoted lines, *"Video meliora, proboque,/ Deteriora sequor"*; so that rather than being implausible or self-contradictory, Moll's recurrent qualms actually emphasize the hold avarice now has upon her.[31]

One could trace the continuation of this process through her subsequent crimes, but it is worth turning directly to her imprisonment in Newgate. Defoe's picture of this "emblem of hell" has been regarded quite rightly as a forcible indictment of contemporary penal conditions, which served to harden criminals more often than reclaim them. His characterization of the Newgate Ordinary, for instance, preaching confession and repentance in the morning, and drunk with brandy by noon, is a powerful expression of reforming indignation. Yet his undeniable concern, here as elsewhere, with the force of external environment does not preclude a more fundamental interest in the spiritual processes taking place within Moll. Throughout the book society is responsible, to a large extent, for her outward vicissitudes, but her own reactions to them give rise to her spiritual predicament. For the latter, she alone is responsible, and to this Defoe devotes the bulk of his attention, even while he is chronicling the horrors of Newgate. In other words, he reports "the hellish noise, the roaring, swearing and clamour, the stench and nastiness, and all the dreadful afflicting things" that Moll sees there, not merely because of the exotic appeal of such a narrative to his respectable readers, which it would surely have, or merely because he regards the place as a foul blemish on

---

[31] The lines from Ovid (*Met.* VII, 20) are quoted by Tillotson in his sermon "Of the Difficulty of reforming Vicious Habits," in *Works*, II, 196.

English justice and humanity, which he clearly does, but because of its hideous effect on the souls of its inmates, who generally enter it in a hardened state only to be further hardened while they remain there. In such a place they seal their damnation, rather than avert it.

Moll's last pseudo-repentance has already been mentioned: soon after she is committed she repents of the crimes that had brought her there, not because they were sinful in themselves, but simply because she was now to suffer for them. We have seen in Crusoe's case that even genuine convictions lead to a sense of helpless despondency, out of which the penitent is rescued only by the intervention of God's grace, and here Moll undergoes a grim parody of the process. Fearing for her neck, not her soul, her convictions are lame. They lead to despair over her bodily, not her spiritual fate, and from this she is rescued, not by God's grace, but by "the indefatigable application of [her] diligent governess," who arranges a delay in her trial. Moll describes the result very vividly, declaring that "I ought to have esteemed it as a space given me for repentance, and have employed it as such, but it was not in me. I was sorry, as before, for being in Newgate, but had few signs of repentance about me.

"On the contrary, like the water in the hollows of mountains, which petrifies and turns into stone whatever they are suffered to drop upon; so the continual conversing with such a crew of hell-hounds had the same common operation upon me as upon other people. I degenerated into stone; I turned first stupid and senseless, and then brutish and thoughtless, and at last raving mad as any of them" (II, 93–94).

The process I have been tracing is thus extended to

its furthest point. Each of Moll's abortive repentances has left increased hardness in its wake, but despite the gradual enslavement of her will, she has retained some capacity to reflect on her actions. Her judicial power has survived her executive power; now, however, that too is lost. She supplements the above confession by recording that "a certain strange lethargy of soul possessed me. I had no trouble, no apprehensions, no sorrow about me . . . my sense, my reason, nay, my conscience, were all asleep. . . . I neither had a heart to ask God's mercy, or indeed to think of it. And in this, I think, I have given a brief description of the completest misery on earth" (II, 94–95). As her very anguish ceases, her spiritual condition becomes completely wretched. With this step, the process of hardening reaches its climax.

The traditional stages of repentance have been examined in previous chapters, and it is unnecessary to recapitulate them here. It is enough to say that when Moll finally does repent, the genuineness of the process is emphasized not only by its contrast with all the insincere and incomplete versions that have preceded it, but also by its conformity to the classic pattern of spiritual rebirth. Consideration was commonly regarded as the first step towards repentance, and long discussions of it were extrapolated from Luke 15:17, "And when he came to himself . . ." (see above, page 107, note 39). In Moll's case, the reunion with her Lancashire husband, and the news that she is to be tried at the next Session, cause her "wretched boldness of spirit" to abate. "I began to think," she says, "and to think indeed is one real advance from hell to heaven. All that hardened state and temper of soul . . . is but a deprivation of thought; he that is restored to his thinking, is restored to himself" (II, 97).[32] Her consideration does not merge directly into conviction, however; when one of the keepers advises her to prepare for death, she is still not brought, as she puts it, "to any sense of being a miserable sinner, as indeed I was, and of confessing my sins to God, and begging pardon for the sake of Jesus Christ" (II, 99). Nevertheless her reawakening out of utter "lethargy of soul" does make her amenable to the exhortations of the minister who visits her after her trial, and his earnest discourses do evoke genuine convictions in her. She now reviews and laments her past, not merely out of dread of human punishment, but with a sense of having offended God and man, and with a concern for her eternal welfare.[33] The confession that the minister draws from her represents a further phase of her convictions, but the actual culmination of her repentance comes the following morning, with "the excellent discourses of this extraordinary man" again acting as a catalyst. Moll reports that "he revived my heart, and brought me into such a condition that I never knew anything of in my life before. I was covered with shame and tears for things past, and yet had at the

[32] In view of her condition, this may seem a very sanguine notion of what is required for self-restoration, but Moll is describing merely the coming-to-oneself which is the necessary preliminary to repentance; compare Crusoe's description of the same process: "Conscience, that had slept so long, began to awake" (p. 99).

[33] "It was now that, for the first time, I felt any real signs of repentance. I now began to look back upon my past life with abhorrence, and having a kind of view into the other side of time, the things of life . . . began to look with a different aspect, and quite another shape, than they did before" (II, 103).

same time a secret surprising joy at the prospect of being a true penitent, and obtaining the comfort of a penitent—I mean the hope of being forgiven" (ii, 105). We may recall Crusoe lifting his heart as well as his hands up to heaven, "in a kind of ecstasy of joy," upon discovering the text of Acts 5:31, and affirming that "from this time I began to have hope that God would hear me." Moll's joy and hope are of the same kind. We have seen that Defoe tends to describe conversion in a rather subdued manner, and that by his time, few besides Baptists and Quakers retained the old enthusiastic way of revelling in the transports of rebirth. It should be stressed again, however, that this wariness of presumption and cant on the part of Anglicans and conservative Nonconformists implies no lessening of the importance attached to conversion, and no real change in the conception of it. The difference is essentially one of style or tone, with a decorous restraint moderating the jubilant excesses of the past.

Moll's regeneration is portrayed in far less detail than Crusoe's. In the first chapter we stated as a kind of structural law of spiritual autobiography that the greater the attention paid to events before conversion, the less the emphasis given to what happens afterwards, and vice versa. A work that traces in detail the progress of sin, with conversion finally snatching the sinner from the very jaws of hell, will rarely have much to say about subsequent trials or relapses, and this is the case in *Moll Flanders*.[34] While conversion

---

[34] The indications of Moll's altered spiritual state may be noted briefly. For one thing, the references to being hurried on by Fate which marked her earlier career now give way to acknowledgments of the existence and goodness of Provi-

supplies the point of view of the narrator, and the resolution towards which the narrative itself moves, the main substance of the narrative is the spiritual decay that makes repentance ever more necessary, but ever more difficult. By now it should be clear that conversion can provide the organizing principle of a narrative, most of which actually runs directly counter to it. There is a similar paradox in many novels and plays that have marriage as their organizing principle, yet whose actual content consists mainly of the delays and obstructions besetting the ultimately happy pair. In much the same way, conversion can give thematic orientation to a chronicle of sin and hardening, these being the delays and obstructions peculiar to it.

The spiritual evolution I have traced not only helps to account for the apparent inconsistency of Moll's "moral scruples" but also affords grounds for ques-

---

dence. More subtle is the equation Defoe creates between two kinds of new life, the one physical or geographical, the other spiritual. Thus even when Jemmy is arguing against going to Virginia, and finds "the passage into another state much more tolerable at the gallows" (ii, 119), the pun helps to suggest the fundamental change which transportation can involve: sailing from England to America is comparable to passing through death from this life to another. Again, Moll's arguments in favor of transportation more directly contribute to the equation, especially when she speaks of living "as new people in a new world," and of launching out "into a new world, as I may call it." As she uses it, the term is not merely a geographical cliché: the change of surroundings can and should be matched by a change of heart on the part of the transported convicts. It is true that in the "Author's Preface" (p. xxiv) we are told that Moll "lived, it seems, to be very old, but was not so extraordinary a penitent as she was at first." This follows a return to the *Old* World, however, and is qualified by the remark that "indeed she always spoke with abhorrence of her former life, and of every part of it." Although the completeness of her regeneration is called into question, the genuineness of her conversion is not.

tioning certain graver criticisms of the book. The episodic nature of the plot, with all its abruptnesses and discontinuities, has led many critics to doubt the presence of any coherent initial plan on Defoe's part, or of any internal consistency in the action itself. My response to this has been that a work may possess thematic coherence despite any amount of incoherence in the outward narrative, and that a conventional pattern of spiritual decay supplies this coherence in *Moll Flanders*. In the second place, various critics have found Moll's own character as uneven as the story of her adventures: what she is has seemed as inconsistent as what she does. This view has been countered with evidence that many apparent ambiguities or self-contradictions in her character are owing not to any "double vision" on Defoe's part, but rather to a traditional conception of the sinner's progress, which Moll's portrayal largely embodies.

If my arguments do lessen the force of some recent criticisms of *Moll Flanders*, other difficulties remain. I have suggested, for instance, that the achievement of a balance between narrative and spiritualization may be the most basic criterion of literary merit that one can apply to spiritual autobiographies. Since *Moll Flanders* owes much to the autobiographical tradition, it is appropriate to inquire how well the book satisfies this norm. My opinion is that the two elements are not so fully in equilibrium as in *Robinson Crusoe*, but that narrative has not yet outstripped spiritualization as drastically as in some of Defoe's other fiction. As we have seen, a good deal of the narrative in *Robinson Crusoe* requires no explicit "improvement": many of the episodes possess conventional spiritual overtones, so that Defoe need not define their significance. In *Moll Flanders*, on the other hand, most of the actions have no traditional metaphoric meaning, so that their implications have to be spelled out by the narrator. This is managed less arbitrarily than in certain genuine autobiographies, but there is a baldness about some of Moll's commentary that *Crusoe* generally avoids through its use of symbolic action and deft allusion. It is better, after all, for spiritual meaning to be embedded in the narrative itself than to be attached to the narrative through interpretative labels. Thus the lack of actions that carry in themselves familiar, well-defined spiritual significance may place *Moll Flanders* at a certain disadvantage relative to *Robinson Crusoe*.

A more basic departure from the convention of spiritual autobiography is that some portions of the narrative are not spiritualized at all, either implicitly or explicitly; or, at any rate, they are not fully assimilated into the spiritual framework which has been described. We have seen that the impulse to narrate an event for its own sake is latent even in the true spiritual autobiography, although there it tends to be repressed by the demand for spiritual significance. What we find in *Moll Flanders* is that this impulse sometimes has its way: other strains in the heredity of the book assert themselves along with—and contrary to—the autobiographical one. Despite the presence of a thematic pattern which is firm and coherent, there are various passages to which it does not extend. As comments on woman's role in society, as reflections on commerce, crime, and colonization, or simply as gobbets of "narrative realism," many of these passages have an undeniable vitality of their own. At the same time, their very effectiveness tends to obscure the structural integrity which, as I have tried to show, the book as a whole does possess.

Roxana

There is much in *Roxana* that departs from the conventional spirit and shape of autobiography, yet the norms of spiritual autobiography help to bring out some of the book's strengths and weaknesses. The very fact of first-person narration, for instance, poses serious problems of interpretation. In *Moll Flanders,* as we have seen, wicked actions can be narrated and morally "improved" in the first person, since the narrator's point of view is that of a penitent: between the time of committing her misdeeds and the time of writing about them, Moll has undergone conversion. Even in the baldest Newgate confession, the malefactor can comment as well as narrate in his own voice with some show of plausibility, because repentance has intervened. But what is to be done when the subject of the story is *not* snatched at last as a brand from the burning? A book like Bunyan's *Life and Death of Mr. Badman* probably represents the most effective solution. In *Grace Abounding,* Bunyan can describe and deplore his own early sinfulness because his point of view is that of the convert, but in *Mr. Badman* he resorts to third-person narration and commentary. Since Mr. Badman dies impenitent, he cannot chronicle his own misdeeds, or at any rate cannot plausibly moralize about them. Therefore Bunyan invents Mr. Wiseman and Mr. Attentive, whose shared point of view is emphatically regenerate, as narrators and commentators on Mr. Badman's career. Precisely because they are regenerate men themselves, they can present evildoing in all its circumstantial detail, and yet animadvert on each item with due rigor.

Roxana is more or less caught between the positions of Moll Flanders and Mr. Badman. Her moral reflections are fairly numerous, and imply a penitent outlook at the time of writing; in other words, such passages presuppose a regenerate narrator such as Moll Flanders. On the other hand, Roxana is in fact more like Mr. Badman, for she really does harden into final impenitency. Even the "repentance" alluded to in the final sentence of the book seems intended as an ironic confirmation of the fact, as we shall see, not a negation of it. In any event the resulting point of view is highly equivocal: Roxana frequently sounds like Moll, but the force of her moralizing is seriously impaired by her essential similarity to Mr. Badman.

There are several ways of accounting for this difficulty. One hypothesis might be that Defoe set out to portray a process of hardening, as in *Moll Flanders*, with every intention of bringing Roxana to eventual repentance, but at some point decided to let her spiritual development complete its natural course, and end with the distinct prospect of damnation. Another explanation might be that he conceived Roxana as more or less a Badman-figure from the outset; that having chosen to put the story in her own mouth, he was at a loss to insert the required moral interpretation of Mr. Wiseman and Mr. Attentive; that he injudiciously elected to make Roxana her own commentator; and that by this expedient he not only deprived her reflections of much of their intrinsic validity but made her entire character extremely ambiguous. Both views challenge the stature of the book, and a case could be

made for either one. The second, however, seems to
me nearer the truth. I believe there are fairly early
indications that Defoe means to consign Roxana to the
devil, and I believe further that the technical difficulty
of making an unregenerate malefactor her own critic is
the book's undoing. Yet I feel that a crippling tactical
error, rather than mere incompetence, is to blame: had
Bunyan made his villain a first-person narrator, Mr.
Badman would have been in the same predicament
despite all Bunyan's skills.

Roxana's spiritual development has obvious similarities to the early careers of Crusoe and Moll; her
hardening in sin is marked, in fact, by many of the
same symptoms. In the first place, she flouts Providential chastisements and deliverances. For instance, when
the kindly Dutch merchant helps her elude the scheming Jew, she makes the following comment: "And
now Amy and I were at leisure to look upon the
mischiefs that we had escaped; and had I had any
religion or any sense of a Supreme Power, managing,
directing, and governing in both causes and events in
this world, such a case as this would have given
anybody room to have been very thankful to the
Power who had not only put such a treasure into my
hand, but given me such an escape from the ruin that
threatened me; but I had none of those things about
me."[1] She does feel gratitude towards the merchant,

[1] *Roxana*, I, 137. In connection with this passage it is worth
quoting Dottin's observation that in *Roxana* "De Foe s'est
abstenu de répéter ses dissertations favorites sur le rôle de la
Providence et des impulsions secrètes" (*Daniel De Foe*, p.
742). Clearly this is no mere oversight on Defoe's part. We
have seen that until her conversion Moll says nothing about
Providence, but a great deal about "fate" and the devil;
Roxana's failure to allude to Providence is to be traced to the
same cause.

but he is her "deliverer" only "as far as relates to second causes": she fails to look beyond second causes to the first cause of her preservation, and in doing so she is guilty, as earlier chapters have shown, of a kind of practical atheism. Soon afterwards she and her maid Amy sail from Rouen to Rotterdam, and both of them undergo "storm-repentances" of the familiar kind. Roxana is somewhat less terrified by the storm than Amy, but the maid's agonies of conscience gradually infect the mistress, who knows herself to be the cause of Amy's ruin. Both have "serious considerations," suffer "dreadful apprehensions," and form "abundance of resolutions," yet the storm fails to provoke effectual repentance in either of them. As Roxana acknowledges, "the danger being over, the fears of death vanished with it; ay, and our fear of what was beyond death also. Our sense of the life we had lived went off, and with our return to life our wicked taste of life returned, and we were both the same as before, if not worse" (1, 145). In this scene, then, Roxana not only thwarts the Providential design in the storm, but shows other familiar symptoms of hardening: she is prone to "considerations" and "reflections" which are neither deep nor durable, and leave her more callous than before, and she is subject to insincere and incomplete repentances which likewise leave only greater hardness in their wake.

Other instances of these latter features may be noted briefly. When Roxana decides to break off her arrangement with the lord who has kept her for eight years, she experiences some "just reflections upon me relating to things past, and to the former manner of my living," yet as she goes on to admit, "there was not the least hint in all this from what may be called religion or conscience, and far from anything of repentance, or anything that was akin to it" (II, 15). Her other bouts of serious consideration are equally remote from repentance, just as her so-called repentances are themselves parodies of its true nature. In addition to the "storm-repentance," which proves shallow and fleeting, she has several penitential seizures resembling Moll's first one in Newgate, which are defective because they spring from mere dread of punishment rather than from genuine detestation of sin. For instance, when Roxana has finally married her devoted merchant, and is about to leave with him for Holland, she begins to look upon her "gay and wicked course" with abhorrence. Yet she confesses that "I was not come to that repentance that is raised from a sense of Heaven's goodness; I repented of the crime, but it was of another and lower kind of repentance, and rather moved by my fears of vengeance, than from a sense of being spared." At the very end of the book, when she falls into "a dreadful course of calamities" after "some few years of flourishing and outwardly happy circumstances," she somberly concludes that "I was brought so low again, that my repentance seemed to be only the consequence of my misery, as my misery was of my crime." [2]

The discrepancy between true repentance and these partial or debased versions of it would be clear from the preceding chapter, even if we did not have Rox-

[2] II, 86, 167; cf. also Roxana's fuller comment on the storm-repentance (I, 145–46), which might serve equally as a gloss on Moll's first Newgate-repentance. Various critics have found the conclusion of *Roxana* unsatisfying, and the final paragraph is indeed perplexingly abrupt: I therefore cite it as a passage consistent with, but not crucial to, my interpretation of the heroine's spiritual fortunes.

ana's word for it. But apart from these indirect indications of hardening, there are other ways in which her spiritual career resembles Moll's. In fact, she is guilty of much the same sins, for the vanity and avarice that characterize Moll are equally pronounced in her. When she is courted by the Prince, her vanity is inflamed by his lofty compliments: "This was the way in all the world the most likely to break in upon my virtue, if I had been mistress of any; for I was now become the vainest creature upon earth, and particularly of my beauty, which as other people admired, so I became every day more foolishly in love with myself than before." [3] Avarice also gains a firm hold over her. Like Moll, she pleads the irresistible force of poverty in extenuation of her initial lapse, but acknowledges that "excess of avarice for getting money and excess of vanity continued me in the crime" (II, 17). Thus at the end of three years as the King's mistress she takes one of her periodic inventories, and finds she has grown rich beyond the dreams of avarice—or as she puts it, "even avarice itself seemed to be glutted" (I, 207). Yet like Moll, who cannot leave off her "trade" even when she has become rich, she continues to be prompted by avarice, and before long is being kept by a "person of honour" who has the further and more essential qualification of being a "person of great estate" (I, 208).

This brief catalogue of traits would imply that Rox-

[3] I, 67; cf. Roxana's assertion that "though poverty and want is an irresistible temptation to the poor, vanity and great things are as irresistible to others" (I, 70). And when she has rejected the Dutch merchant's offer of marriage, she confesses to having "a thousand wild notions in my head that I was yet gay enough, and young and handsome enough, to please a man of quality"; as a result, "blinded by [her] own vanity," she resolves to try her fortune at London, "come of it what would" (I, 183).

ana's spiritual predicament is very similar to Moll's. Why, then, should one suppose that her serious reflections and false repentances, her admissions of vanity and avarice—in short, all her moralizing passages—are any less plausible or consistent than Moll's? Does the difference in effect depend solely on the fact that Moll is ultimately converted, while Roxana is not? If this were all, it could be objected that Defoe need only have added a final repentance scene to salvage Roxana's consistency, and retroactively legitimate her moralizing. Yet the fact is that there are features of her hardening that have no real parallel in *Moll Flanders*, traits that align her more closely with Mr. Badman and his ilk and that rule out, in Defoe's mind at least, the feasibility of a last-minute conversion. To be sure, he and his contemporaries believed that God can reclaim the vilest of sinners up to the very moment of death, but they also believed that God can be provoked, as one divine expresses it, "to give the sinner up to the way of his own heart, and seal his condemnation." [4] As we have seen, this was regarded as the real danger of hardness of heart, and Defoe probably intended to illustrate it in the case of Roxana. The evidence for this is now to be considered. Whether or not it bears out conclusively my suggestion that Defoe regarded his heroine as a damned soul, it at least helps to explain why he might have balked at making her end as a redeemed penitent.

We have seen that the relationship between reason and morality is developed with some care in *Moll Flanders*. On the one hand, Moll's reason continues to generate "moral scruples" up to the time of her commitment to prison. Even though her will is enslaved by

[4] Ryther, *Plat for Mariners*, p. 59; cf. Wright, *Deceitfulness of Sin*, p. 86; cf. also p. 58 n. 8 above.

persistence in sin, the light of conscience is extinguished only by the final lethargy of soul that Newgate induces. On the other hand, we are shown that reason unsupported by religious conviction is inadequate either as a guide or guardian to morality: Moll is repeatedly "reasoned out of her reason" by the devil's advocates, and her reason is similarly overcome by the force of her own opposed inclinations. In *Roxana*, the vicissitudes of reason play an even more important part. They not only illustrate the early stages of hardening more clearly than the traits already considered, but they point up degrees and dimensions of hardening which are simply not found in Moll.

Roxana's story, like Moll's, really begins with a seduction, yet the submission to her landlord has deeper affinities with Moll's first theft. The outward plights of the two women are obviously similar, in that both are isolated and defenceless victims of poverty. More important, neither one is blind to the wickedness of her deed, pleas of necessity notwithstanding. From Roxana we get explicit admissions that "I did what my own conscience convinced me, at the very time I did it, was horribly unlawful, scandalous, and abominable" (1, 40), and that "I sinned with open eyes, and thereby had a double guilt upon me" (1, 46). The same point emerges more subtly from the long preliminary discussions between Roxana and her maid. For instance, there is the pleasant irony of Amy's argument that Roxana cannot justly deny the landlord anything: "Has he not brought you," she asks, "out of the devil's clutches, brought you out of the blackest misery that ever poor lady was reduced to?" [5] As was shown in

[5] 1, 38; that the irony will not be lost, Defoe makes Roxana exclaim soon afterwards. "Why, you argue for the devil, as if

Moll Flanders, poverty does expose its victims to the devil's "baits and snares"; nevertheless one actually falls into his clutches only through succumbing voluntarily to his temptations. The landlord's generosity, like the very poverty it wards off, may be a bait to the devil's hook, yet it is through an act of her own will that Roxana gives herself up to the devil (1, 40). At any rate, she sums up this incident as follows: "So with my eyes open, and with my conscience, as I may say, awake, I sinned, knowing it to be a sin, but having no power to resist. When this had thus made a hole in my heart, and I was come to such a height as to transgress against the light of my own conscience, I was then fit for any wickedness, and conscience left off speaking where it found it could not be heard" (1, 47).

Although Roxana's conscience does flare up on subsequent occasions, she is portrayed in the main as someone whose conscience actually has "left off speaking." Far from being torn between the dictates of reason and inclination, she becomes an apologist for her inclinations; far from being discomfited by conscience, she strives to quell it in others. What happens to her is well described in a sermon by Archbishop Tillotson. "At his first setting out in a wicked Course," Tillotson argues, the sinner "offends against the Light of his own Mind, and does wickedly when he knows better: yet after he hath continued for some time in this Course, and is heartily engaged in it, his foolish

---

you were one of his privy councillors" (1, 39), and he supplements this with Roxana's observation that "The ignorant jade's argument, that he had brought me out of the hands of the devil, by which she meant the devil of poverty and distress, should have been a powerful motive to me not to plunge myself into the jaws of hell, and into the power of the real devil, in recompense for that deliverance" (1, 40).

Heart is darken'd, and the Notions of Good and Evil
are obscured and confounded, and things appear to
him in a false and imperfect Light: His Lusts do at
once blind and byass his Understanding; and his Judgment by degrees goes over to his Inclinations. . . .
He is now engaged in a Party, and factiously concerned to maintain it, and to make the best of it; and to
that end, he bends all his Wits to advance such principles as are fittest to justifie his wicked Practices." [6] Or,
as Joseph Caryl has expressed it a generation earlier, in
his survey of the stages in hardening, the sinner comes
to appear "a Patron, an Advocate for sin, who was before but a practicer of it." [7]

The first evidence of this tendency on Roxana's part
is the scene in which she puts her maid to bed with her
landlord. At this stage her notions of good and evil are
not yet "obscured and confounded," but she is hardened enough to want others to share her guilt: "I was
now become the devil's agent, to make others as
wicked as myself . . . [I] encouraged them both,
when they had any remorse about it, and rather
prompted them to go on with it than to repent it" (I,
51). As she comes to take the devil's part so actively, it
is natural that her judgment "by degrees goes over to
[her] Inclinations," and that she should learn to
"justifie [her] wicked Practices." Her next liaison,
with the Prince, reveals this gradual blinding and
biasing of her understanding: she observes of this affair

[6] "Of the Difficulty of Reforming Vicious Habits," in
Works, II, 196–97; cf. Joseph Hall, *The First Century of
Meditations and Vows*, No. LX, in *Works*, VII, 452; E[dward]
Young, "The Progress of Sin," in *Sermons on Several Occa-
sions*, 3rd edition, 2 vols. (1720), I, 3–4.
[7] *Exposition . . . of Job*, I, 763.

that the devil "played a new game with me, and prevailed with me to satisfy myself with this amour, as a lawful thing" (1, 75), and she goes on to confess that "I was the easier to persuade myself of the truth of such a doctrine as this when it was so much for my ease and for the repose of my mind to have it be so" (*ibid.*).

This kind of "ease and repose" involves a degree of hardening which Moll attains only in Newgate. The very language used to describe it is the same, for Roxana wonders "at the stupidity that my intellectual part was under all that while; what lethargic fumes dozed the soul" (1, 76). The difference, of course, is that Moll has no further scruples once she reaches this stage, while Roxana continues to have periodic disturbances of conscience, and her "intellectual part" remains wakeful. As a consequence, her hardening fails to obey an orderly progression, or at any rate lacks some of the gradual, cumulative quality that traditionally characterizes the process. An explanation for this departure from convention has already been suggested: Defoe wants to indicate that her soul reaches a fairly desperate condition early in her career, but since he has made her the narrator of her own story, she herself must continue to supply its "improvement." Whether the moral responses are ascribed to Roxana the immediate participant or to Roxana the reflective narrator, there is a loss of consistency and plausibility. On the one hand, she is perfectly orthodox in her observation that it is possible "for us to roll ourselves up in wickedness, till we grow invulnerable by conscience; and that sentinel, once dozed, sleeps fast, not to be awakened while the tide of pleasure continues to flow, or till something dark and dreadful brings us to ourselves again" (1, 76). On the other hand, we have seen what it actually means to be brought to oneself again. This never happens to Roxana, yet her "intellectual part" stays active.

A partial resolution of this paradox is to be found in the nature of her ensuing reflections, for instead of being upsurgings of conscience, they tend more and more to be rationalizations that put conscience to rest. Like the old governess in *Moll Flanders*, Roxana becomes adept at reasoning people out of their reason; or, as Tillotson had expressed it, she bends all her wits to advance such principles as are fittest to justify her wicked practices. Indeed this is one of the most interesting features of the book, since there are probably few greater sophists in fiction than Roxana.

At first, as we should expect, she has too clear a notion of right and wrong to deceive herself: it is Amy who acts the casuist in the opening scene of the book, and although Roxana's will is swayed, she never gives her moral assent to Amy's specious arguments. In the scene just considered, however, Roxana persuades herself that her amour with the Prince is lawful. She comments that "I had no casuists to resolve this doubt," and toys with the idea of stating her case to a priest, but eventually manages—without the help of "any of the Romish clergy"—to keep her conscience from giving her "any considerable disturbance in all this matter." In short, she becomes a capable casuist herself.[8]

This development culminates in her long debate

---

[8] "Casuist" is here used in its pejorative sense, but casuistry of a more reputable kind—as developed by Perkins, Baxter, Taylor, Sanderson, and others—figures prominently in many of Defoe's works.

with the Dutch merchant over matrimony. In stating
the case for female independence, Roxana has struck
several critics as very "modern" in outlook. Thus
Aitken felt that her argument "might have been taken
from some of the novels of to-day," while Dottin
found her theories "*hardies et très modernes*," and saw
Roxana herself as "*l'ancêtre peu respectable des
suffragettes*." [9] But she in turn has a long, and not
altogether respectable, ancestry. Calista, the heroine of
Nicholas Rowe's popular and influential "she-
tragedy," *The Fair Penitent* (1703), sounds remarkably like Roxana when she declares,

> How hard is the Condition of our Sex,
> Thro' ev'ry State of Life the Slaves of Man?
> In all the dear delightful Days of Youth,
> A rigid Father dictates to our Wills,
> And deals our Pleasures with a scanty Hand;
> To his, the Tyrant Husband's Reign succeeds:
> Proud with Opinion of superior Reason,
> He holds Domestick Bus'ness and Devotion
> All we are capable to know, and shuts us,
> Like Cloister'd Idiots, from the World's Aquaint-
>   ance,
> And all the Joys of Freedom. Wherefore are we
> Born with high Souls, but to assert our selves,
> Shake off this vile Obedience, they exact,
> And claim an equal Empire o'er the World? [10]

[9] Aitken, introduction to *Roxana*, p. xi; Dottin, *Daniel De
Foe*, p. 745. Cf. also Bernbaum, *Mary Carleton Narratives*,
p. 23.

[10] Act III, Scene 1, in *Dramatick Works*, 3 vols. (1733), II, 30.
The writings of Mary Astell are cited as a possible source of
Roxana's argument in Spiro Peterson's valuable article, "The
Matrimonial Theme of Defoe's 'Roxana,'" *PMLA*, LXX
(1955), p. 186, n. 45.

Calista's plea for female liberty is more impassioned than Roxana's, and no elaborate reasoning is offered in its support, yet the drift of the two is fundamentally the same. There is no proof, of course, that Roxana, as a "Patron and Advocate for sin," is directly descended from Rowe's heroine. Her lineage may extend much farther back in time, to "that woman Jezebel" whose crime was not merely to live loosely herself, but "to teach and to seduce my servants to commit fornication." The passage from Revelation may seem very remote from the world of Roxana; however uncertain its contribution to her feminist genealogy, it does at least help to clarify her spiritual condition. Although her overt deeds are scarcely more criminal than those of Moll Flanders, there is the important difference that while Moll seeks prey, Roxana seeks proselytes. While Moll is drawn to commit sins, Roxana actively avows them; like Jezebel, Roxana is guilty not merely of fornication but of preaching and promoting it.

In other words, it seems to me quite mistaken to regard the debate between Roxana and her Dutch merchant simply as an extreme statement of Defoe's characteristic feminism. I have already noted passages in *An Essay upon Projects* and *Moll Flanders* in which Defoe insists on the legitimate rights of women. Parallels could be cited from his other works, such as *Religious Courtship* and *The Great Law of Subordination Considered*, and, to look no farther afield, there is an instance earlier in *Roxana* of his concern for women's hazards in matrimony (cf. the discussion of fools as husbands, 1, 4–5). Nevertheless he makes an important distinction between grievances and aspirations that are just and those which are vain or wicked. He consistently maintains that wives deserve certain prerogatives, but since his aim is to reform and strengthen the institution of marriage, not to abolish it, he stresses the freedom and dignity that can and should attend it, and virtually denies that a woman can obtain them otherwise. We have seen that Crusoe's attempt to achieve liberty in defiance of family, social and divine order is punished with enslavement, both literal and figurative, while the eventual acknowledgment of dependence results in an actual enlargement of his scope and power of action. Roxana's arguments in favor of female freedom are as misguided as Crusoe's flight: in Defoe's view the submissive acceptance of responsibility is not only compatible with, but indispensable to, genuine liberty. As the merchant is forced to admit, Roxana supports her theories with "subtle reasoning," yet we need not assume that Defoe endorses a position simply because he presents it as vigorously as possible. His own view of the matter is probably reflected in the merchant's protest. "Dear madam," he exclaims, "you argue for liberty, at the same time you restrain yourself from that liberty which God and nature has directed you to take, and, to supply the deficiency, propose a vicious liberty, which is neither honorable or religious." Roxana herself not only comes to dismiss her sophistry as "platonics," and to acknowledge the foolishness and wickedness of her position, but she states at the very outset of the discussion that she is prompted only by the fear of losing her money. "I was obliged to give a new turn to it," she says, "and talk upon a kind of elevated strain, which really was not in my thoughts, at first, at all; for I own . . . the divesting myself of my estate and putting my money out of hand was the sum of the matter that made me refuse to marry." [11]

[11] I, 179; II, 52; I, 180; I, 167. There is a reprise of this discussion in the interview with Sir Robert Clayton (I, 194–95),

Whatever the antecedents of Roxana's brand of feminism, it does serve to reveal the state of her soul: she is not only "engaged in a Party," to use Tillotson's words, but she is "concerned to maintain it, and to make the best of it." Even at this stage, of course, she is still hypothetically within the reach of redeeming grace. If she is denied this, however, her only remaining steps can be despair and damnation. Clearly she does not proceed directly to despair and damnation: on the contrary, she returns to London, which proves to be the scene of new splendors and triumphs. Nearly a decade, in fact, passes between Roxana's rejection of the merchant in Rotterdam and her marriage to him in London, and this period is full of gratifications to her vanity and her avarice. But her character remains static; grow worse she cannot, repent she will not. Chances to alter her course are frequently presented, but her power to seize them is gone. Thus she asserts at one point that "I had so long habituated myself to a life of vice, that really it appeared to be no vice to me," with the result that "I went on smooth and pleasant" (I, 214). It is at this era that she acquires the romance-

---

who tells Roxana that she speaks "a kind of Amazonian language."

In Part III of *Religious Courtship* Defoe draws a very clear distinction between "liberty of conscience" and "liberty without conscience"; the maid Mary's plea for "liberty" resembles Roxana's, and is even more obviously culpable (pp. 226, 229). In an early poem Defoe argues that "Restraint from Ill is Freedom to the Wise" (*A New Discovery of an Old Intreague*, in *A Second Volume of the Writings of the Author of the True-Born Englishman* [1705], p. [5]); he quotes this line years later, in one of his investigations of true and false liberty in *Applebee's Journal* (see William Lee, *Daniel Defoe: His Life and Recently Discovered Writings*, 3 vols. [1869], II, 426; cf. II, 353; II, 479).

name "Roxana," and this is in some ways the most romance-like portion of the story. It is also the most superficial, not because more goes on in the outward narrative than elsewhere in the book, but because less goes on within Roxana herself. Nor is it merely that she ceases to change or develop, although this is the case, but rather that her overt actions have such small bearing on her inward state: the narrative assumes a momentum of its own, and does little to affect or illuminate Roxana's own nature. Towards the end of the book, however, her character is put in motion once again. I have suggested that she can move very little farther in the path she has chosen: unless she is to reverse her direction completely through repentance, despair and damnation are the only remaining stations on her route.

It would be an overstatement to say that the prevailing tone of Roxana's later years is one of despair, if only because uninflected narrative continues to outweigh its "improvement." Yet from the time of her marriage to the Dutch merchant, the story begins to strike a more somber note. This is not owing merely to the shift in outward scene, from the gay opulence of Pall Mall to the subdued domesticity of a Quaker home in the City; after all, Roxana does acquire both an English and a Dutch title. It has to do rather with the gloomy foreboding which Roxana begins to experience, and the air of increasing despondence that marks her thoughts. At the prospect of joining her ill-gotten wealth to the merchant's fortune, she reports that "I trembled every joint of me, worse for aught I know than ever Belshazzar did at the handwriting on the wall" (II, 84). She becomes apprehensive about "the justice of heaven, which I had reason to expect would some time or other still fall upon me or my effects, for the dreadful life I had lived." [12] She denies that this marriage makes her happy or easy, for "there was a dart stuck into the liver; there was a secret hell within" (II, 85; cf. Daniel 5:6 and *passim*). Moreover, she declares that "I had such constant terror upon my mind, as gave me every now and then very terrible shocks, and which made me expect something very frightful upon every accident of life.

"In a word, it never lightened or thundered, but I expected the next flash would penetrate my vitals, and melt the sword (soul) in this scabbard of flesh; it never blew a storm of wind, but I expected the fall of some stack of chimneys, or some part of the house, would bury me in its ruins; and so of other things" (II, 85; cf. Proverbs 7:23).

Once settled in Holland, she and her spouse lead "a very regular, contemplative life; and, in itself, certainly, a life filled with all human felicity." Nevertheless she affirms that serious reflections tend more and more "to prey upon my comforts, and lessen the sweets of my other enjoyments. They might be said to have gnawed a hole in my heart before; but now they made a hole quite through it: now they ate into all my pleasant things, made bitter every sweet, and mixed my sighs with every smile" (II, 89, 90). As a consequence, she reports, "I grew sad, heavy, pensive, and melancholy; slept little, and ate little; dreamed continually of the most frightful and terrible things imaginable: nothing but apparitions of devils and mon-

---

[12] II, 85; the reference to God's justice falling upon her effects is less an expression of materialistic morality than of her fears for the merchant, whose own wealth, she argues, may be jeopardized by being mixed with hers.

sters, falling into gulfs, and off from steep and high precipices, and the like" (II, 90). At this point the long story of Roxana's daughter is inserted: once more the narrative bounds to life, but again Roxana's inward development is arrested. Only in the final sentences of the book do we get another glimpse of her spiritual state, a glimpse that tends to confirm the pattern of spiritual decay I have traced, despite the allusion to repentance.

In any event, the foregoing statements suggest that Roxana sinks into despair. Allusions to the books of Daniel and Proverbs, fears of sudden death and other dream-fancies may seem strange in one who has, as we have seen, "so long habituated [herself] to a life of vice, that really it appeared to be no vice." Once again the sheer fact of first-person narration makes for implausibility. But her symptoms would have suggested despair to anyone familiar with the matter, and that many readers did take an interest in it is indicated by the great popularity of Nathaniel Bacon's *Relation of the Fearful Estate of Francis Spira*.[13] It hardly need be said that despair, like the whole process of heart-hardening, is essentially a spiritual condition, involving a loss of confidence in God's mercy, if not its implicit

[13] This went through more than a dozen editions between 1638 and 1700, and gave rise to various imitations, one of them appearing in the same year as *Roxana*. See Thomas Sewell, *A True Second Spira* (1697); and *The Third Spira. Being Memoirs of the Life, as also a Reasonable Account of the Terrible Despair and Death, of a Young English Gentleman at Paris, In the year 1717* (1724). After telling and hearing some anecdotes of despairing sinners, Bunyan's Mr. Wiseman declares that "alas, should I set myself to collect these dreadful stories, it would be easy in little time to present you with hundreds of them" (*The Life and Death of Mr. Badman* [1956], pp. 294–95).

denial. By reducing his heroine to this state, Defoe completes her tragedy, or at least carries it as far as possible. Once again, he may be somewhat handicapped by the fact that Roxana herself is the narrator; this is a tragedy whose ending she can only darkly anticipate. It is not her final assertion that "I fell into a dreadful course of calamities" that makes the book a tragedy, since her outward misfortunes are no more tragic in themselves than her inward agonies. But both point towards a conclusion that *is* tragic. Without introducing Mr. Wiseman and Mr. Attentive, Defoe cannot supply the catastrophe: nevertheless his foreshadowing of Roxana's doom leaves little doubt that she is ultimately damned, and is far more dramatic than any explicit declaration.

I have shown that *Roxana* retains various features of the spiritual autobiography, whose traditional spirit and form were discussed in Chapter I. In spirit, *Roxana* follows autobiographical convention by presenting a regenerate narrator who chronicles and "improves" the course of her soul's development. But this spirit, as we have seen, is violated in two ways. First, Roxana's point of view is not, as it turns out, that of a convert: she eventually provokes God "to give [her] up to the way of [her] own heart, and seal [her] condemnation." Second, there is a great deal of narrative that she simply fails to "improve," narrative that is included on other grounds than its spiritual significance. In form, *Roxana* follows autobiographical convention by presenting a pattern of spiritual decay. But this shape is distended by the inclusion of much spiritually unassimilated narrative; and while such narrative does not directly violate the structure I have traced, its sheer bulk and vitality tend to obscure the somber implications and indeed the very outlines of Roxana's spiritual devolution. The fact that she is not ultimately reclaimed marks a further departure, of course, from the conventional form of spiritual autobiography—a departure which biography can accommodate but which autobiography cannot. It is a departure whose effect, I have suggested, is to make the book a kind of tragedy. Given "space to repent," Jezebel "repented not": such, in short, is Roxana's tragedy, although its potential impact is greatly lessened by ambiguities in the heroine's point of view and by the preponderance of animated but thoroughly untragic narrative.

Spiritual autobiography continues to furnish a narrative technique and a degree of thematic coherence, but narrative itself has become paramount, and largely eludes thematic control. It seems to me that this process is carried still further in Defoe's other works of fiction: *Colonel Jacque*, for instance, preserves distinct vestiges of the spiritual autobiography, but virtually abandons both its characteristic spirit and shape. As a consequence the narrative, despite its great merits, forfeits the coherence of design which I have traced in *Robinson Crusoe* and *Moll Flanders*. We are accustomed to regard these two works as forerunners of a new tradition, that of the true English novel. Yet it is equally important to recognize them as heirs to a long tradition of spiritual autobiography, a tradition that probably reaches its fullest imaginative expression in *Robinson Crusoe*.

Robinson Crusoe *and the* Myth *of* Mammon

What we make of the hero's labors greatly influences our response to *Robinson Crusoe*. Indeed, from Rousseau's day to our own, most differences of interpretation are traceable to this single factor, the varying significance attached to Crusoe's work.[1] One recent commentator, for instance, finds implicit in it the creed of the dignity of labor: on his reading, Crusoe's efforts signify that the human lot is heroic only when productive, and that man is capable of redemption only through untiring labor. "If we draw a moral," this critic maintains, "it can only be that for all the ailments of man and his society, Defoe confidently prescribes the therapy of work."[2]

We may question, however, whether such an interpretation does justice either to Defoe's intention or to the facts of the narrative. The ideology here ascribed to Defoe had found expression long before the

[1] See Charles Eaton Burch, "British Criticism of Defoe as a Novelist, 1719–1860," *E.S.*, Vol. 67 (1932), pp. 178–98, and "Defoe's British Reputation 1869–1894," *E.S.*, Vol. 68 (1934), pp. 410–23.

[2] Ian Watt, "*Robinson Crusoe* as a Myth," pp. 165, 166 and *passim*; *The Rise of the Novel*, pp. 72–74. Cf. Max Weber, *The Protestant Ethic and the Spirit of Capitalism* (N.Y., 1958), pp. 171–72 and *passim*.

appearance of *Robinson Crusoe:* Mammon, after all, is traditionally its most eloquent advocate. It is he who counsels his fellows in Pandaemonium not to attempt further insurrections,

> but rather seek
> Our own good from ourselves, and from our own
> Live to ourselves, though in this vast recess,
> Free, and to none accountable, preferring
> Hard liberty before the easie yoke
> Of servil Pomp. Our greatness will appear
> Then most conspicuous, when great things of small,
> Useful of hurtful, prosperous of adverse,
> We can create, and in what place so e're
> Thrive under evil, and work ease out of plain
> Through labour and endurance.[3]

To be sure, Milton makes clear from the outset that Mammon is "the least erected Spirit that fell from Heav'n"; yet some modern criticism would have us see such a figure in Robinson Crusoe.

In my opinion there is a vast difference in spirit between Mammon, that prototypical *homo economicus,* and the regenerate Crusoe. Before examining Defoe's hero, however, we might glance briefly at *The Faerie Queene,* for in the second book Spenser presents not only Mammon but the opposite extreme, in the figure of Phaedria. In fact, Phaedria's song to Cymochles (II. vi. 15–17) leads us back to an important source of the entire problem, the passage in the Sermon on the Mount (Matthew 6:24–34) in which Christ urges that man take no thought for the

[3] John Milton, *Paradise Lost,* II, 252–62, in *Poetical Works,* edited by Helen Darbishire, 2 vols. (Oxford, 1952), I, 32–33.

morrow. "Ye cannot serve God and Mammon," Christ warns, and Phaedria's song is in its own way a powerful dissuasive from laying up treasures upon earth.[4]

No critic, it is true, identifies Crusoe's island with Phaedria's. But to establish the fact that he is not cast away in Mammon's cave, either, we should consider some other views on the Mammon-versus-Phaedria dilemma, for there are numerous discussions of it during the seventeenth century. These often take the form of discourses on that portion of the Sermon on the Mount which Phaedria has glossed for us, after her fashion. They sometimes occur in sermons on other texts, such as I Peter 5:7, "Casting all your care upon him, for he careth for you," or Philippians 4:6, "Be careful for nothing"; and they frequently appear in practical works other than sermons, notably in treatises on Providence. Occasionally these discussions will crop out even in works of self-examination and meditation, and I shall begin by citing one such instance, since it puts very concisely the usual solution of this dilemma. Bishop Hall declares in the 287th of his *Meditations and Vows, Divine and Moral* that "there is an holy carelessness, free from idleness, free from distrust. In these earthly things I will so depend on my Maker, that my trust in him may not exclude all my labour; and yet so labour, upon my confidence on him, as my endeavour may be void of perplexity." [5] That

---

[4] Phaedria's argument is defective, of course, in its failure to advise instead that one lay up treasures in heaven. She agrees with Christ in repudiating "fruitlesse toile," but differs greatly in her motive for doing so: namely, her conviction that man should "present pleasures chuse." Moreover, she appeals to the sheer abundance of nature, rather than the fact of divine provision, as grounds for casting off care.

[5] *Works*, VII, 515; cf. No. 126, VII, 467.

idleness was anathema to the seventeenth-century English mind we have been told sufficiently; a point we tend to lose sight of is that distrust was to be just as carefully avoided. If divines of that era seem to have had ringing in their ears God's sentence on the fallen Adam, "In the sweat of thy face shalt thou eat bread, till thou return unto the ground" (Genesis 3:19), they were equally conscious of Christ's words in the Sermon on the Mount.

When they called attention to this paradox, they did so in order to show that the alternatives were not in fact mutually exclusive. Like the relation of faith to works as a basis for salvation, labor and dependence on God came to be regarded as a "both/and," not an "either/or" relationship. Just as true faith, far from obviating works, would be productive of them, so the right kind of dependence on God, far from ruling out human effort, would give it impetus and sanction. The two problems were frequently treated as analogous, and resolved in much the same way: thus Thomas Lye, one of the preachers at Dr. Annesley's Cripplegate Exercises, observes that "As faith shows itself by its works (James 2:18), so trust discovers itself by its obedience, especially in the use of such means as God prescribes for the bringing about his appointed end. . . . God's means are to be used, as well as God's blessing to be expected." [6] There is little suggestion here that one claim takes precedence over the other, let alone that the two are antagonistic. Both obligations are binding, but each is qualified by the other: Christ had not countermanded God's bidding, but had amplified it, had ordered man to go about his tasks in a

[6] "How are we to live by faith on divine providence?" in *Cripplegate Exercises*, I, 374.

new spirit. Even though God fully determines the outcome of every action, man is expected to cooperate; he is responsible for the performance, if not for the result. As one writer says, "The use of means in matters, is Man's work; the Issue or success of means, is God's work"; or as another remarks, "Tho we are sure God has decreed the certain event of such a thing, yet we must not encourage our *idleness*, but our diligence." [7]

When Lye and others spoke of "the use of means," they frequently wanted to stress that God not only compels man to exert himself, but guides and assists him in his exertions. Stephen Charnock, an Emmanuel-trained Presbyterian writing in the 1670's, is typical in asserting that Providence "directs us by means; not to use them is to tempt our Guardian; where it intends any great thing for our good, it *opens* a door, and puts such circumstances into our hands, as we may use without the breach of any Command, or the neglect of our Duty." [8] The splendid thing about Providence, in the eyes of such writers, is not that it simply "provides" for man, but rather that it affords him—if he is attentive and obedient to its dictates—the means of providing for himself. Thus Providence does not excuse man from action, but calls him to it and sustains

[7] T[homas] C[rane], *Isagoge*, p. 475; Stephen Charnock, *Works*, p. 531. See Edward Synge, *A Gentleman's Religion* (1700), pp. 173–74; Jeremy Collier, *Several Discourses upon Practical Subjects* (1725), pp. 103–04; and John Tillotson, "The Necessity of Supernatural Grace, in order to a Christian Life," in *Works*, VIII, 506.

[8] Charnock, *Works*, p. 531; cf. Samuel Scattergood (1646–1696), *Fifty-Two Sermons, Upon Several Occasions*, 2 vols. (Oxford, 1810), I, 173; Benjamin Whichcote, *Works*, I, 359–60; John Tillotson, "The Wisdom of God in his Providence," *Works*, VI, 409.

him in it. Richard Sibbes, whose *Soul's Conflict* (1635) Walton piously bequeathed to his son, insists that "We must not put all carelessly upon a providence, but first consider what is our part; and, so far as God prevents us with light, and affords us help and means, we must not be failing in our duty. We should neither outrun nor be wanting to Providence." [9] Nearly a century later, Defoe himself was to assert that "To be utterly careless of ourselves, and talk of trusting Providence, is a lethargy of the worst nature; for as we are to trust Providence with our estates, but to use, at the same time, all diligence in our callings, so we are to trust Providence with our safety, but with our eyes open to all its necessary cautions, warnings, and instructions." [10] Providence, in short, imposes obligations: it indicates solutions rather than simply performing them, it evokes effective action rather than obviating it, and confers human responsibility rather than precluding it.

All this would tend to refute Phaedria, who makes the bounty of Nature an argument for sloth, but it may seem to guard less effectively against the opposite danger, that of robust Mammonism. We should bear in mind, however, the conviction that just as man must

[9] *The Soul's Conflict with Itself, and Victory Over Itself by Faith*, in *Complete Works*, I, 209. Cf. [Richard Allestree], "Of Trust in God," in *The Whole Duty of Man*, Sunday I, Par. 55. The very phrasing is similar in William Burkitt's *The Poor Man's Help, and Young Man's Guide* (N.Y., 1788; 1st edition, 1693), p. 14.

[10] *Serious Reflections*, pp. 190–91; cf. p. 183 and *passim; The Compleat English Tradesman*, 2nd edition (1727), II, 183. See also Samuel Slater, *Cripplegate Exercises*, III, 327–28; John Tillotson, "Success not always answerable to the probability of Second Causes," in *Works*, II, 357; and Lancelot Andrewes, *Ninety-six Sermons*, 5 vols. (Oxford, 1841–43), IV, 68.

heed and apply strenuously the lessons that Providence teaches, so conversely his efforts will be fruitless if he sets about them without a due regard for Providence. Total self-reliance and unaided human labor are regarded as vain, blind, and perverse, since God is never a mere spectator and since, as the preachers were fond of repeating, the race is not to the swift, nor the battle to the strong, neither yet bread to the wise, nor yet riches to men of understanding, nor yet favor to men of skill. Since God can interrupt or deflect the ordinary sequence of cause and effect to work his will in the world, it is both impious and imprudent to rely on one's own efforts and calculations.

It is this end of the stick that was used to beat the followers of Mammon. We have seen Thomas Lye's warning against sloth, that "God's means are to be used, as well as God's blessing to be expected"; his onslaught against Mammon is even more forceful. The man of faith, he says, "leaves it to the atheist in being *fortunae suae faber;* or, with that dunghill wretch who, being excited to thank God for a rich crop of corn, replies, 'Thank God shall I! Nay, rather thank my dung-cart!' " [11] The other divines cited earlier

[11] *Cripplegate Exercises*, I, 383. This attitude was satirized throughout the period; see Francis Quarles's portrait of "The Worldly Man's Verdour," in *Judgement and Mercy for Afflicted Souls* (1646), in *Works*, edited by A. B. Grosart, 3 vols. (Edinburgh, 1880), I, 87. Cf. the merchant's assertions in "Man's Injustice towards Providence" (1713), in *The Poems of Anne Countess of Winchilsea*, edited by Myra Reynolds (Chicago, 1903), pp. 196–98. Finally, the conclusion of Pope's Epistle to Bathurst lies partly within this tradition in such lines as the following:

> Behold Sir Balaam, now a man of spirit,
> Ascribes his gettings to his parts and merit;
> What late he call'd a Blessing, now was Wit,
> And God's good Providence, a lucky Hit.

express similar sentiments, though seldom in such
earthy terms.[12] Moreover, various Biblical texts were
used to support the argument. In a sermon preached
before the House of Commons, William Jane urges his
listeners "not to boast of the arm of flesh, *to sacrifice to
our net, or burn incense to our drag* (Habakkuk 1:16),
or say with the Assyrian (Isaiah 10:13), *By the might
of my hands I have done this, and by my wisdome, for
I am prudent.*" [13] What is to be avoided is the extreme
position of those who, in Samuel Clarke's words, "rely
with such confidence on the Effects of their own
Wisdom and Industry, and so presumptuously depend
upon the natural and regular Tendencies of second
Causes; as if they thought, either there was no Superior
Cause at all, on which the Frame of Nature depended;
or at least, that the Providence of God did not conde-
scend to direct the Events of Things, in this lower and
uncertain World." [14] Industry, then, has no intrinsic

(Epistle III, "Of the Use of Riches," ll. 375–78, in *Epistles to
Several Persons,* edited by F. W. Bateson [1951], p. 120.)

[12] William Gurnal had used the same anecdote some years
earlier, however, in *The Christian in Compleat Armour,* p. 313.

[13] *A Sermon Preached . . . the 26th of November, 1691*
(Oxford, 1691), pp. 8–9; on the texts from Habakkuk and
Isaiah see Edward Waple, *Thirty Sermons,* pp. 139–40, 142;
Thomas Manton, *Sermons* (1678), pp. 267–68; Jeremy Col-
lier, "Of Discontent," in *Essays upon Several Subjects,* Part
III, 3rd edition (1720), pp. 86–87. Compare *The Compleat
English Tradesman,* II, 235; speaking of the way a tradesman
should behave when successful, Defoe says that "To boast of
his own Wisdom in the amassing his Money, and insult the
Senses and Understanding of every Man that has miscarried, is
not only a Token of Immodesty, but . . . 'tis the infallible
Mark of Irreligion; 'tis sacrificing to his own Net, and to his
own Drag, to his own Head, and to his own Hands."

[14] "The Event of Things not always answerable to Second
Causes," in *Sermons,* VI, 187–89. The proper relation between
diligence and dependence had been summed up memorably
by Donne a century earlier in the third verse letter "To The

merit; it becomes valuable only when coupled with an acknowledgment of God's ultimate power to further or thwart it. Mammon's independence and self-reliance, far from being redeeming features, are at the very core of his iniquity, since they involve a denial of God's sovereignty.[15]

This rapid survey would indicate that the seventeenth-century attitude towards diligence and sloth was somewhat more subtle than generally recognized. Instead of lauding the one and castigating the other, preachers and poets alike arrived at a sort of compromise: what they wanted was an alert, active acquiescence, and a humble, resigned striving. It remains to show that Crusoe, following his conversion, comes to fulfill this ideal, rather than the one embodied and proposed by Spenser's and Milton's Mammon. The first thing to consider is Crusoe's behavior be-

---

Countesse of Bedford" (*Poetical Works*, edited by H. J. C. Grierson [Oxford, 1912], p. 173):

> Who prayer-lesse labours, or without this, prayes,
> Doth but one halfe, that's none; He which said, *Plough
> And looke not back*, to looke up doth allow.

Donne alludes to Luke 9:62; John Flavel was to make a similar point in *The Seaman's Companion* (1676), in *Whole Works*, II, 267.

[15] Compare Benjamin Whichcote, "The Conversion of a Sinner," in *Works*, I, 218: "It was never God's intention when he made man at first, to put him into a state of absolute *independency*, or *self-sufficiency*. And therefore whosoever assumes it to himself, doth assume that which never did belong to a creature-state."

Mammon is guilty of that kind of "thoughtfulness for the morrow" that necessarily proceeds, as John Howe expresses it, "from an ungovernable spirit, a heart not enough subdued to the ruling power of God in the world." Howe's treatise "Of Thoughtfulness for the Morrow," first published in 1681, is one of the most systematic explorations of this whole question: see his *Works*, pp. 328–48, esp. p. 333f.

tween his shipwreck and his conversion. With as yet no sense that he is an object either of Providential chastisement or care, Crusoe's initial reaction to his situation is one of despondence. It is noteworthy that until his conversion he calls his new setting the "Island of Despair," and always refers to it as "a horrible desolate island," "this horrid island," "this dismal unfortunate island," or "that wild miserable place" (pp. 76, 69, 72, 85). At the outset, then, he does not see wherever he looks acres that cry out for improvement, nor does he settle down to his task glowing with purposive possession.[16] He does set to work, however, and it is worth examining the nature and results of his labors. Two episodes can be singled out which seem to characterize them all, up to the time of his conversion: the springing up of the barley affords one kind of commentary on his efforts, the partial destruction of his cave by earthquake another.

Near his fortification Crusoe shakes out a grain-bag, in which he sees nothing but husks and dust; after the rainy season he finds barley growing on the spot. Dry husks drove the prodigal back to his father's home, and ten or twelve ears of green English barley nearly have the same effect on Crusoe. At first he takes this for a miracle, and begins to bless himself that such a prodigy of nature should happen on his account; he is ready to acknowledge himself the beneficiary of Providence.

[16] Crusoe is thus in no frame of mind to exclaim, with Mammon,

> This Desart soile
> Wants not her hidd'n lustre, Gemms and Gold;
> Nor want we skill or art, from whence to raise
> Magnificence; and what can Heav'n shew more?

(*P.L.*, II, 270–78; but cf. Watt, "*Robinson Crusoe* as a Myth," p. 162.)

But when he recalls shaking out the bag in that place, he confesses that "the wonder began to cease" and "my religious thankfulness began to abate too, upon the discovering that all this was nothing but what was common." As he goes on to reflect, however, "I ought to have been thankful for so strange and unforeseen providence, as if it had been miraculous, for it really was the work of Providence as to me" (pp. 84–86). In other words, he relapses quickly into what he himself later condemns as an exclusive attention to second causes; he fails to look beyond them to a first cause. He is still like the "dunghill wretch" Thomas Lye spoke of, who attributes a crop to natural causes rather than thanking God for it.[17]

The relation between Crusoe's own efforts and God's doing also emerges clearly from the earthquake episode. With his improvised tools, Crusoe struggles to make his cave "spacious enough to accomodate [him] as a warehouse or magazine, a kitchen, a dining-room, and a cellar." In eight minutes an earthquake threatens to ruin the work of six months. But once again, he fails to see God's hand in the matter. As he later remarks, "though nothing could be more terrible in its nature, or more immediately directing to the invisible Power, which alone directs such things, yet no sooner was the first fright over, but the impression it had made went

[17] On the necessity of distinguishing between "second causes" and a "first cause," see Richard Baxter, *The Divine Life* (1664), in *Practical Works* (1830), XIII, 32; Isaac Barrow, "On the Gunpowder Treason," in *Theological Works* (Oxford, 1859), I, 448–49; Samuel Clarke, *Sermons*, X, 11–12; Joseph Hall, *Works*, VIII, 28–29. Defoe himself frequently deplored, as in the *Review*, I (IX), 2, that "second Causes have the Blessings or Curses of every Action, without any regard to the great first moving Cause of all Things."

off also." [18] Thus he repeats his error over the barley. In the former case, Providence had made the most casual action fruitful; in the latter, Providence negates his most assiduous toils. Each episode minimizes, in a different way, the role of Crusoe's own efforts, and correspondingly magnifies the role of Providence. On both occasions Crusoe frustrates the divine intention, for neither blessing nor alarm brings him to a sense of his dependence on God.

Eventually he does gain this awareness; what happens, in fact, is that the labors of the regenerate Crusoe come to fulfill the wishes of the divines quoted earlier. After conversion he does not slacken his efforts, but goes about them in an altogether different spirit. Recognizing that providence plays a decisive and benign role in all his affairs, he learns thankfulness and resignation. Previously, he reports, "the anguish of my soul at my condition would break out upon me on a sudden, and my very heart would die within me. . . . In the midst of the greatest composures of my mind, this would break out upon me like a storm, and make me wring my hands, and weep like a child" (p. 125). But now, comforted by the Biblical assurance that "I will never, never leave thee, nor forsake thee," Crusoe attains a serenity that no subsequent crises and alarms can long interrupt. It is not the therapy of work that confers this security, but the realization that he is the object of what one bishop calls "that special providence of God, which is man's only security." [19] He gains a sense of well-being, not

[18] Pp. 79, 83, 87, 81, 99; cf. p. 88, where Crusoe says, "All this while I had not the least serious religious thought, nothing but the common 'Lord, have mercy upon me!' and when it was over, that went away too."

[19] George Bull, *Works*, I, 470; cf. Crane, *Isagoge*, pp. 16, 160–61, and 523.

through purposive possession, but through under-standing that God has furnished him a table in the wilderness.[20] What affords him peace of mind is not his success in the role of *homo economicus,* but the dis-covery that he can rely on Providence for direction and support. By making himself amenable to expres-sions of the divine will, by becoming alert and tract-able, he can at once avail himself of divine assistance, and free himself of the immoderate care rebuked in the Sermon on the Mount. If, as Mr. Watt rightly ob-serves, Crusoe "turns his forsaken estate into a triumph," it is less through sheer labor than through acquiring a sense of dependence; and it is this sense of God's concern and provision for him that keeps such a triumph from being, as Mr. Watt finds it, "a flagrant unreality."[21] For, as Coleridge observed long ago, "The carpentering, tailoring, pottery, are all just what will answer his purpose, and those are confined to needs that all men have, and comforts all men desire. Crusoe rises only where all men may be made to feel that they might and that they ought to rise—in reli-gion, in resignation, in dependence on, and thankful acknowledgment of the divine mercy and good-ness."[22]

[20] In three places Crusoe echoes the passage from Psalm 78:19: see pp. 104, 143, 164. Compare also the allusion to Eli-jah and the Ravens (I Kings 17:4–6) at p. 146. In his Auto-biography (1711), Robert Knox meditates on the same text: see *An Historical Relation of Ceylon together With some-what concerning Severall Remarkeable passages of my life that hath hapned since my Deliverance out of my Captivity,* edited by James Ryan (Glasgow, 1911), p. 400.

[21] *"Robinson Crusoe* as a Myth," p. 167.

[22] *Coleridge's Miscellaneous Criticism,* edited by T. M. Ray-sor (Cambridge, Mass., 1936), p. 300.

INDEX

DATE DUE

~~JAN 25 07~~			
JUL 24 1984			
GAYLORD			PRINTED IN U.S.A.